T0290688

The

Norske Nook

Book of Pies

and Other Recipes

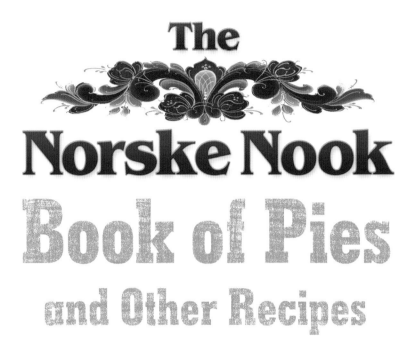

The Norske Nook Book of Pies and Other Recipes

Jerry Bechard
and Cindee Borton-Parker

The University of Wisconsin Press

The University of Wisconsin Press
1930 Monroe Street, 3rd Floor
Madison, Wisconsin 53711-2059
uwpress.wisc.edu

3 Henrietta Street, Covent Garden
London WC2E 8LU, United Kingdom
eurospanbookstore.com

Printed in Korea

Library of Congress Cataloging-in-Publication Data

Bechard, Jerry, author.
  The Norske Nook book of pies and other recipes / Jerry Bechard and
Cindee Borton-Parker.
     pages   cm
  Includes index.
  ISBN 978-0-299-30430-0 (cloth : alk. paper) — ISBN 978-0-299-30433-1
(e-book)
 1. Pies—Wisconsin. 2. Desserts—Wisconsin. 3. Cooking, Scandinavian. 4.
Norske Nook (Restaurant). I. Borton-Parker, Cindee, author. II. Title.
  TX773.B4145   2015
  641.8609775—dc23
                                2014037003

We dedicate this book to all
Norske Nook bakers, past and present

Contents

Introduction

Jerry Bechard

My story with Norske Nook begins where Helen Myhre's leaves off. Helen Myhre is one of the most influential people in my life, and of course at Norske Nook. It was her dedication to her family and passion for quality home cooking that transformed her from a 1960s farm housewife to a successful restaurant owner in the small town of Osseo, Wisconsin. In 1973, she opened the first Norske Nook, in Osseo, and singlehandedly transformed the sleepy little community into a tourist destination. The town also accepted its new role with friendliness and small-town charm, further drawing in the masses.

What were Helen's secrets? She's famous for her dedication and work ethic, but more importantly, she paid such careful attention to the small details of the café. And though she was stern and expected the same dedication from her employees, she also treated her staff with great respect and made them feel like a part of her family.

This work ethic and sense of family would shine through when she cooked her delicious farm-style meals, and of course her wonderful pies. Pies, pies, and more pies! Pies are what transformed Norske Nook from just another hometown café into a world-renowned destination. Pies are what captured

the media's attention and brought the tourists from around the world.

I suppose now you're trying to figure out how I fit into the Norske Nook picture. Well, you could say that working in the restaurant and food service industry is in my blood. My grandfather on my father's side was French Canadian and was a cook in the lumber camps near Chippewa Falls, Wisconsin, at the turn of the twentieth century. My grandfather on my mother's side worked in a bakery in Norway when he was young, before immigrating to the United States.

I grew up on a small farm just outside of Chippewa Falls in the early 1960s. I have many fond memories of the wonderful food at our family gatherings. My mother was in the army nurse training program near the end of World War II, and then became

Osseo

a housewife. She was an extraordinary cook and truly enjoyed baking. She passed her love of food and cooking on to me, though then I was unaware that was happening (my dream was actually to become a policeman). I remember that as a child, I wasn't rushing home off the school bus at the end of the day to get to the freshly baked cakes or cookies, but instead to get to the TV to watch *The Andy Griffith Show* or *Adam-12*. Little did I know, those cookies, cakes, and pies that I enjoyed so much while I watched TV would end up helping me make a living and provide for my own family years later.

After I graduated high school, I attended college at the University of Wisconsin–Eau Claire, and I worked as a manager for a local theater. My supervisor, Gary Joles, and the owner, Gene Grengs, helped me to learn how to be an effective manager and to make decisions and learn from my mistakes, all while serving up buttered popcorn and hot dogs. I was still very focused on getting my degree in law enforcement, but a friend needed help managing a Perkins restaurant in Madison, Wisconsin, and that changed everything. I was tired of working over forty hours a week while carrying a full class load at college, so I decided to give it a try. I attended Perkins's valuable restaurant management training program and began my journey in restaurant management. After working in Madison for six months, I heard that Perkins needed managers in Colorado, and I made the move to Wheatridge, Colorado. I also helped to open a few other stores and worked for a time in Utah. I was the youngest unit store manager they had ever hired, and I really enjoyed it. It was my first taste not only of managing many employees but also of the food service industry. I remember being struck by the amount of pre-prepared food and mixes that were used. My mother had always made everything from scratch.

After a few years in Colorado and Utah, I decided to finish my law enforcement degree. While in school, I got a job working on the bottling line at Coors. When I was twenty-one, I took on a law enforcement job while still finishing my degree. At twenty-three, I was a supervisor and was well on my way with my new career.

I worked for several years in the Denver area, but my wife and I wanted to be back in the Midwest to raise our children. At that time, the late 1980s, the pay scale for a law enforcement job in Wisconsin was not impressive. That's when I stumbled upon an ad in an Eau Claire newspaper about a small-town café for sale. I was interested and, given my law enforcement prospects, decided to inquire.

I contacted the realtor, and he told me it was the Norske Nook, as if surely I had already heard of it, though I hadn't because we'd been out of the area for so long. After hearing him talk about the café, and hearing the cost to buy it, I wondered why the business was for sale at all. The realtor told me that the owner wanted to retire and write a cookbook. I asked family and others in the area about the reputation of the café. They vouched for it and were very surprised that it was for sale. The cost seemed a bit high to me, but I looked at her numbers, which looked great, and decided to go and see it.

But, before I could even make an offer, I needed to sit down for an interview with Helen Myhre, to see if I would fit in and to get her approval. So, I booked a flight to

Wisconsin. I met with my sister-in-law Judy for her help and for a second opinion on the café. I had no idea that this first meeting with Helen, a simple chat over pie, would completely change my life.

We talked for several hours, and I got a feel for her pleasant and motherly nature. And I had my first experience with her pie, which was heavenly. I told her about my background, and she told me the history of the restaurant and about the famous people who would show up at, and return to, her little café. What concerned her the most about handing the restaurant off to a new owner was her

Evelyn Olson (*left*) and Eleanor Holmen (*right*), Osseo

staff. Her employees were like family to her, and she wanted to be sure they'd be in good hands.

After taking a tour of the restaurant and seeing the town of Osseo, I was excited for the opportunity to buy the restaurant. Going from a large city to a small town would be a big change, but one that my family and I welcomed.

I returned home, wondering if Helen would deem me the right person to take over Norske Nook. It was about a week before the realtor called me with the good news, and after six months of finalizing details with him and the bank, Norske Nook was officially mine in October of 1990. Helen agreed to stay on for six months, while she wrote

her book, to help get me trained and acclimated. During this time she also appeared on David Letterman's show, making her famous sour cream raisin pie!

At first I was overwhelmed, learning to cook everything completely from scratch, and cooking enough of it to feed the hundreds of diners that Norske Nook served each day. In the morning I was the prep cook, and I baked breads, cooked roasts, prepared soups, and the like. At eight o'clock Helen and her three bakers would begin making the pies. She patiently taught me her recipes, very few of which were written down. I'd carry with me a small notebook, and when we made a recipe I would jot down notes. I learned how to make a new item every day, and I would go home that night and write my notes in the form of a recipe. That was my life then, day in and day out, just learning Helen's recipes.

Every day we made pies, and every day I took notes from each baker and wrote them out. During this time, not only was I learning new recipes, but I was also forming some important relationships. I am forever indebted to Helen Myhre, Lorraine Eidie, Helen Eid, Shari Brown, Alice Steen, Irene Matz, Maggie Jonas, Marge Pettis, and Flo McMann. Whether they worked full time or part time, they were all patient enough to help train me, a complete greenhorn, and allowed me to be a part of their lives.

Making pie dough is about so much more than just the recipe. From baker to baker, there were variations in ingredients, temperature, everything. They taught me instead how the dough should look and feel, and that had a big impact on me. I learned lessons about cooking and baking that you just won't get from recipes. Baking requires passion for mixing the ingredients in a certain way, and adding patience and love to make a final masterpiece. They used to laugh because I wanted to set a timer to know when the pies would be done. They'd tell me you can simply smell when a pie is done. Just a few short months later, I too would learn to smell a pie's doneness.

It took me a lot of trial and error to learn the right feel of pie dough. I would mix up a single batch each day, and the next day it was my job to roll out the dough from that batch. It was a great way to learn what mistakes I was making and how to correct them. With my persistence, and guidance from Helen and her bakers, it all came together.

My pie crusts were often pretty misshapen, and Helen would ask, "What country are you rolling out today?" It was our joke for many months. They would resemble China, Russia, South America. One day she came in and told me her job must be finished, because I was finally rolling out the whole world.

I was busy working every day, and the days leading up to my first Thanksgiving at Norske Nook passed quickly. I was amazed at the number of pies we made for that Thanksgiving. But my amazement tripled when I witnessed my first summer at the restaurant. Summer is peak tourist season, and I was shocked at the number of people that came in from all over the United States. They'd flock in for breakfast, lunch, and dinner, and almost all of them topped it off with a slice of pie. Then, so many of them would take home a whole pie. I was in awe of the number of pies we were baking daily in our little seventy-five-seat café.

In summer, when we make our strawberry pies, we would clean up to twelve flats of strawberries each day, and often there is a staff member dedicated to just cutting strawberries. And we would *still* run out of strawberry pie. The baking area was small, about sixteen by twenty feet, and there were four of us crammed in there, baking about a hundred pies a day. There was no air-conditioning, and it was incredibly hot with the ovens running all day, but we made it work. We were a well-oiled machine. We also became great friends, sharing our families' news and town gossip while rolling out pie dough and baking pies. Every morning at four thirty, Norske Nook bakers gather to begin making the hundreds of pies we will sell that day, sharing laughs and love along the way.

I was also amazed at the number of people that would line up outside the Norske Nook, waiting their turn to come in and enjoy the pie and friendly service. They came from all over, with smiles on their faces. Each day we served more and more people, some days even exceeding Osseo's own population of fifteen hundred.

We also had our local regulars. They would come early in the morning before the crowds lined up. They also came all winter long when they could enjoy the café without the long lines. We had two "men's" tables

Deedra Nichols (*left*) and Flicka Torpen (*right*), Osseo

Anyway, those long, long lines kept growing, year after year, especially when Helen's book came out. It became clear that we would need to expand. Across the street from the café was an empty lot, which used to be the location of the local hardware store, but it had burned down years earlier. I bought the lot, even though developers and the city thought I might instead want to move out of the old downtown. But I felt that part of the charm of our café was its location in the older section of Osseo. Our original Norske Nook café was part of the heart and soul of downtown Osseo, and we worried what could happen to the small shops that had opened up and were successful because of the traffic that the café brought in. So in the end, the lot across the street was the location for our new restaurant and bakery, and construction began.

and one "women's" table, where world problems were solved over toast and coffee. They'd even come in to tackle important and difficult local issues, never raising a hand in anger, and the discussions ended peacefully. They would often suggest that the government could learn from them if it could come in and negotiate the world's problems over coffee and a slice of pie at the Norske Nook. These groups of regulars are still around today. Some members have passed away, but there are new ones to take their place.

Actually, some politicians have already stopped in to experience our pie and hospitality while campaigning. President Bill Clinton, Newt Gingrich, John Kerry, and Steve Gunderson, to name a few, have dined at Norske Nook. President Barack Obama sent a letter thanking us for Norske Nook pie he enjoyed during a visit to Eau Claire on his campaign tour. They should pass along our local customers' suggestion for the House and Senate to stop in for a pie summit!

Osseo Norske Nook, original location, now a coffee house and gift shop

I kept things the same in the interior, down to the large, hand-painted mural of Norway. But I made the bakery four times larger than it was in the old building. The building was finished, a local minister blessed the stoves, and our doors opened. We turned the old café into a Scandinavian coffeehouse and gift shop, but during the busy summer months we had to keep it open as a restaurant to handle overflow. We now had lines on both sides of the street. With our extra space, we accommodated busloads of tourists. There were tour groups from all over: Japan, Norway, Finland, Poland, and Russia. Many of them didn't speak English, but a smile goes a long way. They would enjoy a meal and a slice of pie, and then many would stand out front and take pictures of each other in front of the restaurant. Some would even hold up their pies like a coveted award.

We had one customer who bought a T-shirt from us, and then traveled around the world, having his picture taken in his Norske Nook T-shirt in front of famous sites like Big Ben, the Kremlin, the Pyramids, the Great Wall of China, and many more. Every three to six months we'd receive another picture from him in front of yet another landmark. We in turn sent him a new T-shirt and gift certificates and told him to spread the word about Norske Nook while on his world travels.

The restaurant was also featured in magazine articles in *Country Today*, *Farm and Ranch*, and *Midwest Living*. There was a nod to our café in Jane and Michael Stern's book *Roadfood*. Articles in newspapers from New York to Los Angeles raved about the pies. With all this recognition came, of course, longer lines and requests for us to open more locations in towns all over the Midwest.

I set out on the road to search for a location where I could open another restaurant. But it needed to be close enough for me to

Osseo Norske Nook, second location

Rice Lake Norske Nook

keep an eye on it. One of my managers in Osseo at that time, Amy Niemen, had grown up in Rice Lake, Wisconsin, a little city on the edge of farms, woods, and water that tourists and families often traveled to for their vacations. I visited the community, met with a developer, and got to know some of the local people. After my visit, I felt the town would be a good fit for a Norske Nook, and we broke ground in the spring of 1995. The new restaurant was welcomed by the community, and it brought more buses and more lines.

Some of the buses that came through Rice Lake were transporting musical acts from place to place for shows and tours. Such acts as Molly and the Haymakers, Los Lobos, Randy Travis, and many others stopped in at Norske Nook for a meal and a slice of pie. Randy Travis wrote us a long letter thanking us for our

pie, saying that only his mother's was better and our pie reminded him of home.

With our new location came a demand for more varieties of pie. The bakers from each location and I came up with new varieties and tested them on family, friends, and customers, receiving rave reviews.

On the heels of opening the Rice Lake location, I decided to take my passion for home brewing to a whole new level. After doing a lot of research, I decided to open a

Osseo's pie case

brewpub in Eau Claire. I had been interested in home brewing since my days in Denver, while working in law enforcement. I made my police buddies the testers for all of my brewing experiments. Northwoods Brewing was born in 1997 and we began brewing many different styles of beer. When locals found out that I was the owner, of course they asked for *pies*. So as not to disappoint them, I added Norske Nook pies to the menu, along with its famous breakfasts and lefse wraps.

It was around this time that we began to contemplate attending the National Pie Championships, sponsored by the American Pie Council. After a lot of soul searching and courage building, we decided to try our luck. We packed our gear, including ingredients, equipment, and pie tins, and headed to Florida, where the competition is held. Once there, we learned that we would have to bake our pies in the motel kitchen, and that our time slot to bake was from 10:00 p.m. to 2:00 a.m. What a challenge that was! Not only were we baking in a completely different kitchen, with unfamiliar ovens and stovetops, but also my regional manager had to leave at 4:00 a.m. to fly back to attend an event for her son. So there I was, all alone, transporting the pies from the motel to the school where the pies would be judged. But it was well worth it in the end, as we won our first blue ribbon there, for our Banana Cream Pie. (Our pies that have won blue ribbons at the championships are identified at their recipes in this book.)

Since that first win, we have attended the National Pie Championships almost every year, and each year the bakers and I come up with even more new recipes. Before

National Pie Championships ribbons

deciding which pies will compete, we test each pie over and over again, and present them to the managers at our quarterly managers' meetings. Each manager votes on the best from each store, and then Cindee Borton-Parker, my regional manager, and I work on getting each pie recipe exactly right, down to the last detail, with help from our bakers. We fine-tune each pie until we feel it is worthy of competing. Then we test them on our regular customers, taking their opinions into account and revising the recipes one final time before the competition. These little "working vacations" also created even stronger bonds among all of us, making a large family out of a group of friends and coworkers as we share our work and our personal stories with one another. Every year we have a great time, not only because we win awards but also because we have fun, working and being together. We could write a separate book about our adventures at the National Pie Championships.

Another great Wisconsin tourist town, Hayward, began asking for a Norske Nook. Never ones to say no to a challenge, we

Marlene Hagen, Osseo

remodeled an existing restaurant in Hayward and opened a third location. And Hayward also has the long lines of customers all summer, everyone wanting a great meal and a slice of award-winning pie. Every day we get another request for a new location, from people who live all over the Midwest, and even in Alaska and Canada. We have even shipped pies to China!

With praise coming in from coast to coast, and requests for the recipes for our newest pie creations, we have decided to write a book to follow up Helen's wonderful work. We could never match her fantastic storytelling, but we'd like to try, and to give our fans some recipes and mouthwatering pictures of our pies. We hope everyone will enjoy the recipes and stories, along with tips and advice from our great bakers, managers, and staff.

I also need to thank Helen Myhre for completely changing

my life, and the hardworking and dedicated staff members I have had the honor of working with, and sharing my life with. There are many who worked with Helen, helped me out in the beginning, and have since retired or passed away. I miss each and every one of them, and the many laughs we shared. I dedicate this book to those who worked with Helen, and all who are still with me—the servers, cooks, dishwashers, hosts, bakers, brewers, bartenders, and managers. Without them, we would not be where we are today. It is through their hard work and dedication that Cindee and I were inspired to write this book. The staff of Norske Nook and Northwoods Brewing have carried on Helen's dream and my dream of making Norske Nook pies a household name.

I'm a pie maker, not really a writer, so I hope I haven't bored you with our story! Without further ado, I present to you the recipes for award-winning pies and more.

Hayward Norske Nook

CRUSTS

Pastry Pie Crusts

Makes two 11-inch, very thin crusts

1 cup all-purpose flour

½ cup butter flavor Crisco

½ teaspoon salt

¼ cup cold water

In a bowl, use your fingers to blend the flour, Crisco, and salt until the mixture becomes crumbly. Add the cold water and mix until smooth. Don't overmix.

Place the dough on a floured table or cutting board. Cover your hands with flour and work the dough back and forth a few times. The dough should hold together when picked up and pressed, and should not crack.

Divide the dough in half and form each half into a nice round ball, about the size of a tennis ball. Set one ball on the floured surface and flatten it into a disk, like a hockey puck. Repeat for the other ball. Wrap each disk tightly with plastic wrap and refrigerate 30 minutes or overnight.

Unbaked Single Crust

When the dough is ready, unwrap it and turn onto a very lightly floured surface. (If the dough is too hard, allow it to sit for 5 minutes to soften.) With a floured wooden rolling pin, roll dough gently, using a back and forth motion from the center, and roll in every direction, turning the dough 45 degrees between each roll to help keep it round. If dough sticks to the work surface, dust lightly with flour. Roll until it is 1 inch larger than the pie tin all the way around.

Transfer the pastry to the pie tin, being careful to avoid stretching it. Trim the pastry to ½ to ¾ inch beyond the edge of the tin. Fold the extra pastry under and crimp it around the edge by using a forefinger from one hand and pinching

the dough next to it between the forefinger and thumb of your other hand. Continue around the edge.

Baked Single Crust

Preheat the oven to 350 degrees.

Follow the directions for Unbaked Single Crust (page 2). With a fork, poke holes in the bottom and sides of the pastry.

Bake for 10 to 15 minutes, depending on your oven, until golden brown. Let cool before adding the filling.

Double Crust

Roll out two disks of dough. Fit one crust in the pie tin and add the filling. Transfer the remaining crust to cover the filling, being careful not to stretch it. Trim the edge and tuck it under the bottom crust; press to seal. Crimp edge of the pastry as described for single crust. Prick with a fork or cut slits with a small sharp knife to allow steam to escape. Bake according to recipe.

For one 11-inch pie

• • • • • • • • • • • • • •

Chocolate Lined Pastry Crust

½ **cup chocolate chips**
1¼ **tablespoons vegetable oil**

Put the ingredients in a saucepan, stir, and melt over medium heat. Spread the mixture over the bottom and the sides of a Baked Single Crust (page 3).

This crust can be used for the Chocolate Mousse (page 154) and Mounds Coconut (page 56) pies.

For one 11-inch pie

• • • • • • • • • • • • • •

Chocolate Peanut Butter Lined Pastry Crust

½ **cup chocolate chips**
¼ **cup peanut butter**
1¼ **tablespoons salted butter**

Put all the ingredients in a saucepan, stir, and melt over medium heat. Spread the mixture over the bottom and the sides of a Baked Single Crust (page 3).

This crust can be used for the Butterfinger (page 61), Chocolate Peanut Butter (page 58), and Snickers Caramel (page 62) pies.

Graham Cracker Pie Crust

For one 11-inch pie

2 cups crushed graham crackers
½ cup powdered sugar
½ cup (1 stick) salted butter, softened

Combine the cracker crumbs and the sugar in a bowl.

Add the butter (butter should be soft, but not melted) and stir to eliminate lumps. Mix, using your fingers, until it becomes crumbly. Be careful not to overmix.

Press the mixture into a pie tin, covering the sides and bottom. When doing the sides you will want to get to the top of the tin.

Refrigerate the crust until fully chilled. Be sure it is well set before adding filling.

Oreo Cookie Pie Crust

For one 11-inch pie

2 cups crushed Oreo cookies
¼ cup (½ stick) salted butter, melted

Place some Oreo cookies in a plastic bag and crush them with a rolling pin as fine as you can. Put the crushed cookies into a small bowl and, using your hands, mix well with the melted butter.

Press the mixture into a pie tin, covering the sides and the bottom. When doing the sides you will want to get to the top of the tin.

Refrigerate the crust until fully chilled. Be sure it is well set before adding filling.

Graham Cracker Crust for Tortes

For one 9-by-13-inch torte

2 cups graham cracker crumbs

1 cup powdered sugar

½ cup (1 stick) salted butter, softened

8 ounces cream cheese, softened

1 cup granulated sugar

1 teaspoon vanilla extract

3 large eggs

Preheat the oven to 350 degrees.

Mix the crumbs and powdered sugar in a bowl. Add the butter and mix until all the butter is incorporated. Spoon the mixture into a 9-by-13-inch baking pan, smooth it out evenly, and press it firmly into the pan.

Put the cream cheese in a bowl for an electric stand mixer, and mix at slow speed to break it up. Add the granulated sugar and vanilla and mix until smooth. Increase the speed to high until the mixture is light and fluffy. Decrease the speed to medium and add the eggs one at a time. Scrape down the sides of the bowl and the bottom. Finish mixing by hand and pour over the graham crust.

Bake for 30 to 35 minutes, until lightly golden brown. Cool on a table or counter. Cover with plastic wrap and refrigerate until ready to use.

Nut Crust for Tortes

For one 9-by-13-inch torte

2 cups all-purpose flour

1 cup pecans, chopped

½ cup (1 stick) salted butter, softened

Preheat the oven to 375 degrees.

Mix all the ingredients in a bowl, using your fingers to mix thoroughly, until crumbly and there are no clumps of butter.

Press the mixture into the bottom of a 9-by-13-inch cake pan and bake for about 20 minutes, until lightly brown and crust has cracks running through. Cover with plastic wrap and refrigerate until ready to use.

Graham Cracker Cheesecake Crust

For one 9-inch cheesecake

1 cup crushed graham crackers

1½ tablespoons salted butter, melted

Place the cracker crumbs in a 9-inch springform pan, make an indentation in the middle, and pour in the butter. Mix crumbs and butter with your fingers and press into bottom of the pan.

Wrap the outside of the pan with aluminum foil, then coat the entire inside edge or ring of pan with a nonstick baking spray.

This crust can be used for the Norske Nook Cheesecake (page 164) and Pumpkin Cheesecake (page 168) recipes.

Oreo Cookie Cheesecake Crust

For one 9-inch
cheesecake

1 cup crushed Oreo cookies

Place some Oreo cookies in a plastic bag and crush them
with a rolling pin as fine as you can. Put the crushed cookies
into the bottom of a 9-inch springform pan.

Wrap the outside of the pan with aluminum foil, then coat the
entire edge or ring of pan with a nonstick baking spray.

This crust can be used for the Chocolate Caramel Cheesecake (page 167) and Orange Dream Pie (page 153) recipes.

TOPPINGS AND PUDDINGS

• •

Cranberry Apple Topping

Makes 5 cups

5 cups Jonathan (or your favorite variety) apples, peeled, cored, and sliced

2½ cups cranberries

½ cup granulated sugar

⅓ cup light brown sugar (not packed)

Pinch of ground nutmeg

½ teaspoon ground cinnamon

⅛ teaspoon salt

⅓ cup water

¼ cup cornstarch

¼ cup cold water

Combine all the ingredients except the last two in a saucepan. Turn heat to high. Stir occasionally until the cranberries start to crack.

Mix the cornstarch and the water to a smooth consistency and add it to the apple-cranberry mixture. Turn the heat to low and simmer for another 15 minutes.

Use this topping on waffles, pancakes, or ice cream.

Dutch Crumb Topping

For one 11-inch pie

1 cup all-purpose flour

¼ cup granulated sugar

½ cup light brown sugar

¾ cup quick-cooking rolled oats

½ tablespoon ground cinnamon

½ teaspoon salt

6 tablespoons salted butter, softened

Preheat the oven to 350 degrees.

In a large mixing bowl, combine the flour, both sugars, oats, cinnamon, and salt. Add the softened (not melted) butter and mix together, using your fingers, until crumbly. Bake as directed in recipe.

Blueberry Topping

Makes 5 cups

2 cups water

3 tablespoons cornstarch

1 cup granulated sugar, divided

4 cups blueberries

Bring the water, cornstarch, and ½ cup sugar to a boil, stirring constantly until clear and thick. Remove from heat.

Add the blueberries and the other ½ cup sugar. Mix thoroughly until thick, and until it reaches a nice blue color.

Use this topping on waffles, pancakes, ice cream, or other desserts.

Butterscotch Pudding

For one 11-inch pie

2 cups packed light brown sugar

3 tablespoons all-purpose flour

3 tablespoons cornstarch

3 large egg yolks

3 cups whole milk

⅓ cup salted butter, melted

1 teaspoon maple flavoring

Put the sugar, flour, and cornstarch into a saucepan and mix well. Add the egg yolks and milk and whisk.

Add the butter and cook over high heat, stirring continuously, until the mixture is thick and boils in the center.

Remove from heat and stir in the maple flavoring.

Lemon Pudding

For one 11-inch pie

2 large egg yolks

3 cups water

Juice and grated rind of 1 lemon

1 cup granulated sugar

3 tablespoons all-purpose flour

2 tablespoons cornstarch

Yellow food coloring

In a medium bowl, beat the egg yolks, water, and lemon juice, and set aside.

In a saucepan, combine the sugar, flour, cornstarch, and grated lemon rind.

Using a whisk, mix the egg mixture and the ingredients in the pan, and cook for 5 minutes over medium heat, until thick and clear. Add a drop of food coloring for extra color.

Chocolate Pudding

For one 11-inch pie

3 cups whole milk

2 (1-ounce) squares bittersweet chocolate

1 cup granulated sugar

3 tablespoons all-purpose flour

3 tablespoons cornstarch

Pinch of salt

1 teaspoon vanilla extract

In a saucepan, combine the milk and the chocolate, and heat until the chocolate melts.

In a small bowl, combine the sugar, flour, cornstarch, and salt. Mix with your fingers.

Gradually add the dry ingredients to the hot milk mixture and stir continuously with a whisk. Cook on medium heat for about 5 minutes, until thick and smooth.

Mix in the vanilla, stir, and remove from heat.

Serve warm with fresh cream or cooled and topped with Fresh Whipped Cream (page 17).

Vanilla Pudding

For one 11-inch pie

1½ cups granulated sugar

¼ cup all-purpose flour

3 tablespoons cornstarch

3 large egg yolks

3 cups whole milk

1 tablespoon salted butter

1 teaspoon vanilla extract

In a saucepan, combine the sugar, flour, and cornstarch, and mix together with a whisk.

Add the egg yolks, but do not mix yet. Gradually add the milk, and stir all together thoroughly.

Cook over medium heat until thick and smooth, stirring constantly with a rubber spatula.

Remove from heat, and add the butter and vanilla. Stir well and cool.

Fresh Whipped Cream

Makes approximately 2 cups

1 cup heavy whipping cream

¼ cup powdered sugar

1 teaspoon vanilla extract

In a large bowl, whip the cream with an electric mixer until stiff peaks start to form. Beat in the sugar and vanilla until peaks form. Be careful not to overbeat or the cream will become lumpy and butterlike.

Lingonberry Topping

Makes 2 cups

2 cups lingonberries, divided

1½ cups granulated sugar

2 tablespoons minute tapioca

1 cup water

¼ cup plus 1 tablespoon cornstarch

¼ cup cold water

Put 1 cup of the lingonberries, all of the sugar and tapioca, and 1 cup of water in a pan and cook on high. Let it come to a rolling boil. Watch it closely so it doesn't boil over.

Mix the cornstarch and cold water to a smooth consistency. When the berry mixture gets to a full rolling boil, add the cornstarch mixture. Turn to low and let it cook for another 10 to 15 minutes.

Remove from heat and add the remainder of the lingonberries.

Use this topping on Norwegian pancakes, French toast, crepes, or ice cream.

DUTCH AND PRALINE-TOPPED PIES

· ·

APPLE TREES TO APPLE PIES

. . . .

I'm very proud of all the pie recipes you will find in this cookbook, from the traditional to the more unusual. There are pies like my mother's and also pies my fellow bakers and coworkers at Norske Nook have helped to create. We wouldn't be where we are now if it wasn't for our creative and hardworking staff along for the ride on our crazy pie adventure!

My mom made such great fruit pies. Her apple and apple crunch pies were the best! We had many apple trees around our house and enjoyed making applesauce and pies from those apples. My brother loved climbing the trees and tossing down the apples. And then there were our apple-throwing wars with those that were rotten and had already fallen. We had brown stains from the splattered apples running down our clothes, and some of those half-rotten apples would even leave a bruise! The apple wars always ended though, and my brother would put his arm around me and we'd walk back to the house with our goodies. Mom would be upset about the apple stains on our clothes, but we'd strip down on the porch and put on clean clothes, and she'd hug us both for bringing home the good apples.

—Jerry Bechard

Dutch Apple Pie

Tip:

For the filling you can substitute a 1-quart jar of Norske Nook Apple Pie Filling.

1 Unbaked Single Crust (page 2)

Topping: Dutch Crumb Topping (page 11)

2½ pounds Jonathan (or your favorite variety) apples, peeled, cored, and sliced

1½ cups granulated sugar

¼ cup all-purpose flour

1 tablespoon cornstarch

1 teaspoon ground cinnamon

Preheat the oven to 375 degrees.

Press the crust into a pie tin and crimp. Place about half the apples in the crust.

In a medium bowl, combine the sugar, flour, cornstarch, and cinnamon.

Sprinkle half the dry mixture over the apples. Add the remaining apples, followed by the remaining dry mixture.

Cover the apples with the topping.

Bake until a knife comes out clear, and not sugary, about 2 hours.

Cherry Crunch Pie

Makes one 11-inch pie

Tip:

For the filling you can substitute a 1-quart jar of Norske Nook Cherry Pie Filling.

1 Unbaked Single Crust (page 2)

Topping: Dutch Crumb Topping (page 11)

2 pounds cherries, pitted

¼ cup cherry gelatin powder

1 cup granulated sugar

2 tablespoons cornstarch

3 tablespoons minute tapioca

1 teaspoon almond extract

Preheat the oven to 375 degrees.

Press the crust into a pie tin and crimp. Place about half the cherries in the crust.

In a medium bowl, combine the gelatin powder, sugar, cornstarch, and tapioca.

Sprinkle half the dry mixture over the cherries. Add the remaining cherries, followed by the remaining dry mixture. Sprinkle with the almond extract.

Cover the cherries with the topping.

Bake until a knife comes out clear, and not sugary, about 2 hours.

Harvest Apple Pie

Makes one 11-inch pie

Tip:

For the filling you can substitute a 1-quart jar of Norske Nook Apple Pie Filling.

1 Unbaked Single Crust (page 2)

Topping: Dutch Crumb Topping (page 11)

2½ pounds Jonathan (or your favorite variety) apples, peeled, cored, and sliced

1½ cups granulated sugar

¼ cup all-purpose flour

1 tablespoon cornstarch

1 teaspoon ground cinnamon

1 cup whole pecans, divided

1 (8-ounce) container frozen whipped topping, thawed, or Fresh Whipped Cream (page 17)

Caramel topping (found with the ice cream toppings at the grocery store) for drizzling

Preheat the oven to 375 degrees.

Press the crust into a pie tin and crimp. Place about half the apples in the crust.

In a medium bowl, combine and mix the sugar, flour, cornstarch, cinnamon, and ¾ cup of pecans. Sprinkle half the dry mixture over the apples. Add the remaining apples, followed by the remaining dry mixture.

Cover the apples with Dutch Crumb Topping.

Bake until a knife comes out clear, and not sugary, about 2 hours. After baking, sprinkle the remaining ¼ cup of pecans over the topping.

Serve with whipped topping or whipped cream and a drizzle of caramel topping.

Blackberry Crunch Pie

Makes one 11-inch pie

1 Unbaked Single Crust (page 2)

Topping: Dutch Crumb Topping (page 11)

2 pounds blackberries
1½ cups granulated sugar
¼ cup all-purpose flour
1 tablespoon cornstarch

Preheat the oven to 375 degrees.

Press the crust into a pie tin and crimp. Place about half the blackberries in the crust.

In a medium bowl, combine the sugar, flour, and cornstarch. Sprinkle half the dry mixture over the blackberries.

Add the remaining blackberries, followed by the remaining dry mixture. Cover with the topping.

Bake until a knife comes out clear, and not sugary, about 2 hours.

Blueberry Crunch Pie

2004 National blue ribbon winner

Makes one 11-inch pie

Tip:

For the filling you can substitute a 1-quart jar of Norske Nook Blueberry Pie Filling.

1 Unbaked Single Crust (page 2)

Topping: Dutch Crumb Topping (page 11)

2 pounds blueberries

1½ cups granulated sugar

2 tablespoons all-purpose flour

1 tablespoon cornstarch

Preheat the oven to 375 degrees.

Press the crust into a pie tin and crimp. Place about half the blueberries inside the crust.

In a medium bowl, combine the sugar, flour, and cornstarch.

Sprinkle half the dry mixture over the blueberries. Add the remaining blueberries, followed by the remaining dry mixture.

Cover the blueberries with the topping.

Bake until a knife comes out clear, and not sugary, about 2 hours.

Peach Raspberry Melba Pie

2010 National blue ribbon winner

Makes one 11-inch pie

1 Unbaked Single Crust (page 2)

3 cups raspberries, divided

1¼ cups granulated sugar

1¼ cups peach gelatin powder

2½ tablespoons cornstarch

1½ tablespoons minute tapioca

2 pounds peaches, peeled, pitted, and sliced

Melba Crumb Topping

1 cup all-purpose flour

½ cup light brown sugar

¼ cup granulated sugar

¾ cup quick-cooking rolled oats

½ teaspoon salt

6 tablespoons salted butter, softened

Preheat the oven to 375 degrees.

Press the crust into a pie tin and crimp. Spread 1½ cups raspberries over the crust.

In a medium bowl, combine the sugar, gelatin powder, cornstarch, and tapioca. Sprinkle half the dry mixture over the raspberries.

Arrange half the peach slices around the outside and then fill to the middle.

Sprinkle the remaining raspberries over the peaches and then sprinkle the remaining dry mixture. Add and arrange the remaining peaches.

To make the melba crumb topping, mix all the dry ingredients in a bowl, then mix in the softened (not melted) butter with your fingers. Sprinkle the topping over the peaches.

Bake until a knife comes out clear, and not sugary, about 2½ hours.

Peach Praline Pie

Makes one 11-inch pie

1 Unbaked Single Crust (page 2)

2½ pounds peaches, peeled, pitted, and sliced

1 cup granulated sugar

2 tablespoons minute tapioca

1 teaspoon almond extract

Praline Topping

1½ cups all-purpose flour

1¼ cups light brown sugar

1 cup pecans, halved

¾ cup (1½ sticks) salted butter, softened

Preheat the oven to 375 degrees.

Press the crust into a pie tin and crimp. Place about half the peaches in the crust.

In a medium bowl, combine the sugar and tapioca. Sprinkle half the dry mixture over the peaches. Add the remaining peaches followed by the remaining dry mixture. Sprinkle with the almond extract.

To make the praline topping, mix the flour, sugar, and pecans in a medium bowl. Mix in the softened (not melted) butter with your fingers. Sprinkle the topping over the peaches.

Bake until a knife comes out clear, and not sugary, about 2 hours.

Jamberry Pie

2014 National blue ribbon winner

Makes one 11-inch pie

1 Unbaked Single Crust (page 2)

Topping: Dutch Crumb Topping (page 11)

2 cups strawberries, quartered

2 cups blackberries

2 cups raspberries

2 cups blueberries

¼ cup raspberry gelatin powder

¼ cup strawberry gelatin powder

1½ cups granulated sugar

2 tablespoons cornstarch

2 tablespoons minute tapioca

Preheat the oven to 375 degrees.

Press the crust into a pie tin and crimp. In a large bowl, mix all of the berries. Place about half the berries in the crust.

In a medium bowl, combine the gelatin powders, sugar, cornstarch, and tapioca.

Sprinkle half the dry mixture over the berries. Add the remaining berries, followed by the remaining dry mixture.

Cover the berries with the topping.

Bake until a knife comes out clear, and not sugary, about 2 hours.

DOUBLE-CRUST PIES

Old-Fashioned Strawberry Pie

2010 National blue ribbon winner

Makes one 11-inch pie

1 Double Crust (page 3)

10 cups strawberries, quartered

1½ cups granulated sugar

7 tablespoons cornstarch

3 tablespoons salted butter, melted

¼ cup sanding sugar (coarsely ground white sugar) for sprinkling

Preheat the oven to 375 degrees.

Place the strawberries in a bowl and add the sugar and corn-starch. Mix well and place the mixture in the crust.

Cover the pie with the remaining crust, crimp around the rim, and cut slits in the top. Brush with melted butter and sprinkle with sanding sugar.

Bake until a knife comes out clear, and not sugary, about 2 hours.

Apple Pie

1 Double Crust (page 3)

2½ pounds Jonathan (or your favorite variety) apples, peeled, cored, and sliced

1½ cups granulated sugar, plus additional for sprinkling

¼ cup all-purpose flour

1 tablespoon cornstarch

Pinch of ground nutmeg

1 teaspoon ground cinnamon

1 tablespoon cold salted butter, cut into 3 slices

Preheat the oven to 375 degrees.

Place about half the apples in the crust.

In a medium bowl, combine the sugar, flour, cornstarch, nutmeg, and cinnamon. Sprinkle half the dry mixture over the apples.

Add the remaining apples, followed by the remaining dry mixture. Dot with the butter slices.

Cover the pie with the remaining crust, crimp around the rim, and prick with a fork or cut slits in the top. Sprinkle with sugar.

Bake until a knife comes out clear, and not sugary, about 2 hours.

Cherry Pie

Tips:

There are two types of cherries—sweet and sour. Sour cherries, also called pie cherries, tart cherries, or tart red cherries, make wonderful pies.

For the filling you can substitute a 1-quart jar of Norske Nook Cherry Pie Filling.

1 Double Crust (page 3)

2½ pounds cherries, pitted

1 cup granulated sugar, plus additional for sprinkling

¼ cup cherry gelatin powder

2 tablespoons cornstarch

3 tablespoons minute tapioca

1 teaspoon almond extract

1 tablespoon cold salted butter, cut into 3 slices

Preheat the oven to 375 degrees.

Place about half the cherries in the crust.

In a medium bowl, combine the sugar, gelatin powder, cornstarch, and tapioca. Sprinkle half the dry mixture over the cherries. Add the remaining cherries, followed by the remaining dry mixture. Sprinkle with the almond extract. Dot with the butter slices.

Cover the pie with the remaining crust, crimp around the rim, and prick with a fork or cut slits in the top. Sprinkle with sugar.

Bake until a knife comes out clear, and not sugary, about 2 hours.

Strawberry Rhubarb Pie

Makes one 11-inch pie

1 Double Crust (page 3)

2 cups granulated sugar, plus additional for sprinkling

½ cup all-purpose flour

3 large eggs

1 teaspoon cornstarch

Pinch of ground nutmeg

2 pounds rhubarb, cut into ¾-inch pieces

2 cups strawberries, halved

1 tablespoon cold salted butter, cut into 3 slices

Preheat the oven to 375 degrees.

Combine the sugar, flour, eggs, cornstarch, and nutmeg in a large bowl and mix well with an electric mixer. Fold in the rhubarb.

Place the rhubarb mixture in the crust, then arrange the strawberries on top. Dot with the butter slices. You will have a very heaping pie, but the rhubarb will shrink considerably when cooked.

Cover the pie with the remaining crust, crimp around the rim, and prick with a fork or cut slits in the top. Sprinkle with sugar.

Bake until a knife comes out clear, and not sugary, about 2 hours. Frozen rhubarb will take longer to bake than fresh.

Mincemeat Pie with Warm Rum Sauce

Makes one 11-inch pie

1 Double Crust (page 3)

Mincemeat Filling

2⅔ cups mincemeat mixture

2 cups Jonathan (or your favorite variety) apples, peeled, cored, and chopped

½ cup granulated sugar, plus additional for sprinkling

1 tablespoon cold salted butter, cut into 3 slices

1 tablespoon brandy

1 tablespoon rum

Warm Rum Sauce

2 cups granulated sugar

4 tablespoons cornstarch

Pinch of salt

3 cups water

¾ cup (1½ sticks) salted butter

¾ cup brandy

½ cup rum

Preheat the oven to 375 degrees.

To make the filling, combine the mincemeat, apples, and sugar and place in the crust. Dot with the butter slices and sprinkle with the brandy and rum.

Cover the pie with the remaining crust, crimp around the rim, and cut slits in the top. Sprinkle with sugar.

Bake until a knife comes out clear, about 1 hour.

To make the rum sauce, combine the sugar, cornstarch, and salt in a saucepan and mix. Add water and boil for 6 to 8 minutes. Remove from heat and add the butter. Stir until butter is melted. Add brandy and rum. Stir.

Serve pie with warm rum sauce drizzled over each slice.

Caramel Apple Pie

Makes one 11-inch pie

1 Double Crust (page 3)

2½ pounds Jonathan (or your favorite variety) apples, peeled, cored, and sliced

1 cup light brown sugar

½ cup all-purpose flour

1 tablespoon cornstarch

½ cup pecans, chopped

1 teaspoon ground cinnamon

½ cup plus 2 tablespoons caramel topping (found with the ice cream toppings at the grocery store)

1 tablespoon cold salted butter, cut into 3 slices

Granulated sugar for sprinkling

Preheat the oven to 375 degrees.

Place about half the apples in the crust. In a medium bowl, combine the sugar, flour, cornstarch, pecans, and cinnamon. Sprinkle half the dry mixture over the apples. Add the remaining apples, followed by ½ cup caramel topping and the remaining dry mixture. Dot with the butter slices.

Cover the pie with the remaining crust, crimp around the rim, and prick with a fork or cut slits in the top. Sprinkle with sugar.

Bake until a knife comes out clear, and not sugary, about 2 hours.

After the pie is baked, drizzle top crust with 2 tablespoons caramel topping.

Peach Pie

Makes one 11-inch pie

Tip:

For the filling you can substitute a 1-quart jar of Norske Nook Peach Pie Filling.

1 Double Crust (page 3)

2½ pounds peaches, peeled, pitted, and sliced

1 cup granulated sugar, plus additional for sprinkling

1 cup peach gelatin powder

2 tablespoons cornstarch

3 tablespoons minute tapioca

1 teaspoon almond extract

1 tablespoon cold salted butter, cut into 3 slices

Preheat the oven to 375 degrees.

Place about half the peaches in the crust.

In a medium bowl, combine the sugar, gelatin powder, cornstarch, and tapioca. Spread half the dry mixture over the peaches. Add the remaining peaches, followed by the remaining dry mixture. Sprinkle with the almond extract, and dot with the butter slices.

Cover the pie with the remaining crust, crimp around the rim, and cut slits in the top. Sprinkle with sugar.

Bake until a knife comes out clear, and not sugary, about 2 hours.

Rhubarb Pie

Makes one 11-inch pie

1 Double Crust (page 3)

2 cups granulated sugar, plus additional for sprinkling
⅓ cup all-purpose flour
3 large eggs
Pinch of ground nutmeg
2½ pounds rhubarb, cut into ¾-inch pieces
1 tablespoon cold salted butter, cut into 3 slices

Preheat the oven to 375 degrees.

Combine the sugar, flour, eggs, and nutmeg in a large bowl and mix well with an electric mixer. Fold in the rhubarb.

Place the rhubarb mixture in the crust and dot with butter slices. You will have a very heaping pie, but the rhubarb will shrink considerably when cooked.

Cover the pie with the remaining crust, crimp around the rim, and prick with a fork or cut slits in the top. Sprinkle with sugar.

Bake until a knife comes out clear, and not sugary, about 2 hours. Frozen rhubarb will take longer to bake than fresh.

Peach Berry Pie

Makes one 11-inch pie

1 Double Crust (page 3)

2 pounds peaches, sliced

1 cup blueberries

1 cup cranberries

1½ cups granulated sugar

¼ cup all-purpose flour

2 tablespoons cornstarch

½ teaspoon salt

½ teaspoon ground nutmeg

1 teaspoon vanilla extract

1 tablespoon cold salted butter, cut into 3 slices

Preheat the oven to 375 degrees.

In a large bowl, combine all fruit and toss to mix. Place about half the fruit in the crust.

In a medium bowl, combine the sugar, flour, cornstarch, salt, and nutmeg. Sprinkle half the dry mixture over the fruit. Add the remaining fruit followed by the remaining dry mixture. Sprinkle with the vanilla extract and dot with the butter slices.

Cover the pie with the remaining crust, crimp around the rim, and cut slits in the top. Sprinkle with sugar.

Bake until a knife comes out clear, and not sugary, about 2 hours.

Cranberry Apple Pie

1 Double Crust (page 3)

2 pounds Jonathan (or your favorite variety) apples, peeled, cored, and sliced

½ pound whole cranberries

1½ cups granulated sugar, plus additional for sprinkling

½ cup light brown sugar (not packed)

½ cup all-purpose flour

2 tablespoons cornstarch

1 tablespoon minute tapioca

1 teaspoon ground cinnamon

1 tablespoon cold salted butter, cut into 3 slices

Preheat the oven to 375 degrees.

Place about half the apples and half the cranberries in the crust.

In a medium bowl, combine both sugars, flour, cornstarch, tapioca, and cinnamon.

Sprinkle half the dry mixture over the apples and cranberries. Add the remaining apples and cranberries followed by the remaining dry mixture. Dot with the butter slices.

Cover the pie with the remaining crust, crimp around the rim, and prick with a fork or cut slits in the top. Sprinkle with sugar.

Bake until a knife comes out clear, and not sugary, about 2 hours.

Blueberry Pie

....

2008 National blue ribbon winner

Makes one 11-inch pie

● ● ● ● ● ● ● ● ● ● ● ● ● ●

1 Double Crust (page 3)

2¼ pounds blueberries

1½ cups granulated sugar, plus additional for sprinkling

¼ cup all-purpose flour

1 tablespoon cornstarch

1 teaspoon brandy

1 teaspoon lemon juice

1 tablespoon cold salted butter, cut into 3 slices

Preheat the oven to 375 degrees.

Place about half the blueberries in the crust.

In a medium bowl, combine the sugar, flour, and cornstarch. Sprinkle half the dry mixture over the blueberries. Add the remaining blueberries, followed by the remaining dry mixture.

Combine the brandy and lemon juice and sprinkle over the pie. Dot with the butter slices.

Cover the pie with the remaining crust, crimp around the rim, and prick with a fork or cut slits in the top. Sprinkle with sugar.

Bake until a knife comes out clear, and not sugary, about 2 hours.

Norwegian Berry Pie

1 Double Crust (page 3)

½ pound cranberries

½ pound lingonberries

1¼ pounds blueberries

2 cups granulated sugar, plus additional for sprinkling

¼ cup all-purpose flour

3 tablespoons cornstarch

1 tablespoon cold salted butter, cut into 3 slices

Preheat the oven to 375 degrees.

In a large bowl, combine all the fruit and place about half the mixture in the crust.

In a medium bowl, combine the sugar, flour, and cornstarch. Sprinkle half the dry mixture over the fruit. Add the remaining fruit, followed by the remaining dry mixture. Dot with the butter slices.

Cover the pie with the remaining crust, crimp around the rim, and cut slits in the top. Sprinkle with sugar.

Bake until a knife comes out clear, and not sugary, about 2 hours.

Lingonberry Apple Pie

Makes one 11-inch pie

1 Double Crust (page 3)

2 pounds Jonathan (or your favorite variety) apples, peeled, cored, and sliced

½ pound (2 cups) lingonberries

1½ cups granulated sugar, plus additional for sprinkling

½ cup loosely packed light brown sugar

½ cup all-purpose flour

2 tablespoons cornstarch

1 tablespoon minute tapioca

1 teaspoon ground cinnamon

1 tablespoon cold salted butter, cut into 3 slices

Preheat the oven to 375 degrees.

Place about half the apples and half the lingonberries in the crust.

In a medium bowl, combine both sugars, flour, cornstarch, tapioca, and cinnamon. Sprinkle half the dry mixture over the fruit. Add the remaining apples and lingonberries followed by the remaining dry mixture. Dot with the butter slices.

Cover the pie with the remaining crust, crimp around the rim, and prick with a fork or cut slits in the top. Sprinkle with sugar.

Bake until a knife comes out clear, and not sugary, about 2 hours.

CANDY PIES

It's always such an honor to attend and compete at the annual National Pie Championships in Celebration, Florida, in April. Every year, the Norske Nook team gets together to share pie ideas and sample pies. We vote on our favorites and prepare the chosen pies for the competition. We make them over and over, making small changes here and there until the pie is perfect. Hard work and dedication like this can only come from a team that shares a passion for pies.

My sister Judy has retired in Florida, about an hour south of where the competition is held. She's been a true lifesaver, letting us store our baking supplies year after year. One time, the oven in our rental house broke, and she let us bake the pies for the competition at her house. In the first years, I think she looked forward to our arrival, but I hope she doesn't change her mind after what we've put her through (what happens in Florida stays in Florida?)! We are very thankful for her help.

—Jerry Bechard

Mounds Coconut Pie

2012 National blue ribbon winner

Makes one 11-inch pie

1 Chocolate Lined Pastry Crust (page 3)

1 batch of Chocolate Pudding (page 16), cooled

4 ounces cream cheese, softened

1 cup powdered sugar

2 (8-ounce) containers frozen whipped topping, thawed (1 for filling and 1 for topping)

4 cups shredded sweetened coconut, plus ½ cup for garnish

8 pieces of fun-size Mounds candy

In a large bowl, beat the cream cheese with an electric stand mixer, add the sugar, and mix until smooth. Fold in one container of whipped topping and mix a bit longer. Add 4 cups coconut and continue mixing by hand, using a rubber spatula.

Spread the filling in the crust and cover with the pudding.

Top the pudding with the other container of thawed whipped topping, sprinkle with the remaining coconut, and arrange the candy, 1 piece per slice of pie. Keep refrigerated.

Chocolate Mint Pie

2006 National blue ribbon winner

Makes one 11-inch pie

1 Oreo Cookie Pie Crust (page 4)

1 batch of Chocolate Pudding (page 16), cooled

4 ounces cream cheese, softened

1 cup powdered sugar

⅛ cup crème de menthe syrup

Green food coloring

1 (8-ounce) container frozen whipped topping, thawed and divided

1 cup crushed Andes mint candy pieces, divided

In a medium bowl and using an electric stand mixer, mix the cream cheese, powdered sugar, crème de menthe syrup, and 1 drop of food coloring. Fold in half the whipped topping and half the candy pieces.

Spead the filling in the crust and cover with the pudding.

Stir 1 drop of food coloring into the remaining whipped topping and spread over the pudding. Sprinkle with the remaining candy pieces. Keep refrigerated.

Chocolate Peanut Butter Pie

2009 National blue ribbon winner

Makes one 11-inch pie

1 Chocolate Peanut Butter Lined Pastry Crust (page 3)

1 batch of Chocolate Pudding (page 16), cooled

4 ounces cream cheese, softened

⅔ cup creamy peanut butter, plus 1 tablespoon for topping

1 cup powdered sugar

1 (8-ounce) container frozen whipped topping, thawed and divided

¾ cup chopped Reese's Peanut Butter Cups

4 Reese's Peanut Butter Cups, cut in half, for garnish

In a large bowl, mix the cream cheese, ⅔ cup peanut butter, and powdered sugar with an electric stand mixer. Fold in half the whipped topping and the chopped Reese's Peanut Butter Cups.

Spread the filling in the crust and cover with the pudding.

Blend together the remaining half of the whipped topping and 1 tablespoon of peanut butter. Cover the pudding with the topping and garnish with Reese's Peanut Butter Cups. Keep refrigerated.

Butterfinger Pie

2007 National blue ribbon winner

Makes one 11-inch pie

1 Chocolate Peanut Butter Lined Pastry Crust (page 3)

8 ounces cream cheese, softened

½ cup creamy peanut butter

1 teaspoon vanilla extract

2 cups powdered sugar

1 (16-ounce) container frozen whipped topping, thawed, plus additional for garnish (optional)

2 cups crushed Butterfinger candy, plus additional for garnish (optional)

In a medium bowl, mix the cream cheese, peanut butter, and vanilla with an electric stand mixer until smooth. Add the powdered sugar and mix again until smooth. Add the whipped topping and mix just a bit more.

Remove the bowl from the mixer, add the candy, and mix by hand with a rubber spatula.

Mound the mixture into the crust. Keep refrigerated.

Serve with more whipped topping and/or candy pieces, if desired.

Snickers Caramel Pie

2010 National blue ribbon winner

Makes one 11-inch pie

1 Chocolate Peanut Butter Lined Pastry Crust (page 3)

8 ounces cream cheese, softened

¼ cup creamy peanut butter

¼ cup caramel topping (found with the ice cream toppings at the grocery store)

1 teaspoon vanilla extract

2 cups powdered sugar

1 (16-ounce) container frozen whipped topping, thawed

2½ cups crushed Snickers candy, divided

Beat the softened cream cheese in a medium bowl with an electric stand mixer. Add the peanut butter, caramel topping, and vanilla and mix. Add the powdered sugar and mix until smooth.

Remove the bowl from the mixer and add the whipped topping. With a rubber spatula, continue mixing by hand. Add 2 cups of the candy and mix thoroughly by hand.

Spread the filling in the crust. Top with remaining ½ cup of the candy. Keep refrigerated.

Kaffe Mocha Pie

....

2013 National blue ribbon winner

Makes one 11-inch pie

● ● ● ● ● ● ● ● ● ● ● ● ● ●

1 Oreo Cookie Pie Crust (page 4)

2 tablespoons flavored ground coffee

8 ounces cream cheese, softened

4 tablespoons whole milk

2 cups marshmallow cream

2 tablespoons chocolate syrup, plus additional for drizzling

1 (16-ounce) container frozen whipped topping, thawed and divided

8 chocolate-covered espresso beans for garnish (optional)

Dissolve 2 tablespoons of your favorite flavored coffee in 2 tablespoons of boiling water. Let steep for 5 minutes. Strain and set aside.

In a medium bowl, whip the cream cheese, milk, and marshmallow cream with a stand mixer until smooth. Add the coffee and chocolate syrup and mix. Fold in 12 ounces of whipped topping.

Mound the filling into the crust. Drizzle with chocolate syrup, and swirl with a knife.

Fill a piping bag with the remaining whipped topping and make 8 dollops in a circle on top of the pie.

Garnish with chocolate-covered espresso beans, if desired. Keep refrigerated.

BERRY PIES

Strawberry Pies on the Head

I will always remember one particular day during my first years as owner of the Norske Nook. I was at the original location, which had a very small bakery area. It was a Friday, and Shari Brown and I were very busy making tons of strawberry and raspberry pies to get ready for the busy weekend ahead. We ran out of space in our bakery cooler, so we decided to stack some pies in the large walk-in cooler. If I remember correctly, there were at least twenty other cream pies stacked around, anywhere we could find room—on top of dressings and pickle jars. I was balancing three finished strawberry pies, each weighing eight pounds, on my hands and arms, and our dishwasher Brian opened the cooler door for me. I walked in and bumped a pie that was stacked on an overhead shelf, and I'm sure you can guess what happened next. It fell on my head and caused a domino effect of pies falling all over me and everywhere. It was not a great day, but it sticks in the memory of all who were there!

—Jerry Bechard

Raspberry, Blackberry, or Strawberry Pie

Makes one 11-inch pie

Tip:

While in most cases fresh fruit is best, we suggest using frozen berries or firm store-bought berries for this recipe. The pie will keep much better.

1 Baked Single Crust (page 3)

Strawberry/Raspberry Glaze

3¾ cups water

2¼ cups granulated sugar

7 tablespoons (3-ounce box) raspberry gelatin powder

7 tablespoons (3-ounce box) strawberry gelatin powder

6 tablespoons cornstarch

3 tablespoons cold water

9 cups raspberries, blackberries, or strawberries

1 (8-ounce) container frozen whipped topping, thawed, or Fresh Whipped Cream (page 17)

To make the glaze, combine the water and the sugar in a saucepan and boil for a few minutes until sugar is dissolved completely. Add the gelatin powders and stir until the mixture boils again.

Dissolve the cornstarch in cold water (start with 3 tablespoons water and add more if necessary to make it smooth). Add it quickly to the above mixture and turn down the heat to simmer, stirring slowly until clear bubbles form, about 5 minutes. Cool until thick, about 30 minutes in the refrigerator.

Place the cooled glaze in a large bowl and mix until smooth. Fold the raspberries, blackberries, or strawberries into the glaze, coating all the fruit and trying not to smash the fruit.

Mound the mixture into the crust. Refrigerate the pie.

Serve with whipped topping or whipped cream.

CREAM CHEESE PIES

Peaches and Cream Pie

2014 National blue ribbon winner

Makes one 11-inch pie

1 Baked Single Crust (page 3)

Topping: Dutch Crumb Topping (page 11)

Peach Filling

2½ pounds peaches, peeled, pitted, and sliced

1½ cups granulated sugar

6 tablespoons peach gelatin powder

6 tablespoons cornstarch

5 tablespoons cold water

Cream Cheese Filling

8 ounces cream cheese, softened

2 cups powdered sugar

1 (8-ounce) container frozen whipped topping, thawed

To make the peach filling, place peaches, sugar, and peach gelatin powder in a saucepan on medium heat and cook, stirring occasionally.

In a small bowl, mix the cornstarch with cold water to make smooth. When the filling comes to a boil and is soft in the center, thicken it with the cornstarch mixture and cook until the cornstarch is cooked clear. Set aside until cooled completely.

To make the cream cheese filling, use the whip attachment of a stand mixer at medium speed to beat the cream cheese and powdered sugar until smooth. Fold in the whipped topping and mix well. Spread the filling in the baked crust.

Spread the Dutch Crumb Topping on an ungreased cookie sheet and bake for 10 minutes. Stir it, turn the pan, and bake for an additional 10 minutes, or until golden brown.

When the fruit filling is cool, mound it on top of the cream cheese filling, then cover completely with the baked Dutch Crumb Topping.

Maple Raisin Pie

....

2010 National blue ribbon winner

Makes one 11-inch pie

• • • • • • • • • • • • • •

1 Baked Single Crust (page 3)

Maple Raisin Filling

1¼ cups light brown sugar

1 cup cook-and-serve vanilla pudding powder

1 tablespoon cornstarch

1 tablespoon all-purpose flour

2 large egg yolks

3 cups whole milk

1 cup shredded or flaked sweetened coconut, plus ½ cup
for garnish (optional)

2 cups raisins, plus additional for garnish (optional)

1 teaspoon maple flavoring

Cream Cheese Layer

8 ounces cream cheese, softened

2 cups powdered sugar

2 (8-ounce) containers frozen whipped topping, thawed
(1 for filling and 1 for topping)

To make the maple raisin filling, in a saucepan over medium
heat, thoroughly mix together the brown sugar, pudding
powder, cornstarch, and flour. Add the egg yolks, milk, coconut, and raisins, stirring continuously until thick. Add the
maple flavoring, stir, and cool completely in refrigerator.

To make the cream cheese layer, use an electric stand mixer
to combine the cream cheese and powdered sugar and mix
until smooth. Add 1 container of whipped topping and mix.
Spread mixture evenly over the bottom of the crust.

Spread the cooled maple-raisin filling over the cream cheese
layer and top with the other container of whipped topping.

If desired, place about ½ cup shredded coconut in a pie pan
under the broiler for just a couple of minutes, watching
closely and stirring occasionally, until golden brown, and
sprinkle over top of pie with chopped or diced raisins.

Coconut Pineapple Dream Pie

2008 National blue ribbon winner

Makes one 11-inch pie

1 Baked Single Crust (page 3)

8 ounces cream cheese, softened

2 cups powdered sugar

1 (16-ounce) container frozen whipped topping, thawed and divided

2 (4.3-ounce) boxes cook-and-serve vanilla pudding powder

2 cups shredded sweetened coconut, plus ½ cup for garnish (optional)

4 cups whole milk

1 (20-ounce) can crushed pineapple, drained

With an electric stand mixer, mix cream cheese and sugar until smooth. Fold in half the whipped topping and mix a bit longer. With a rubber spatula, continue mixing by hand.

Spread the filling into the bottom of the baked crust.

In a saucepan over high heat, cook together pudding powder, coconut, and milk until thickened and center is boiling. Transfer to a plastic bowl and refrigerate.

When pudding mixture is cooled, add pineapple and mix. Mound the mixture over the cream cheese layer. Top with the rest of the whipped topping or Fresh Whipped Cream (page 17). Keep refrigerated.

If desired, place about ½ cup shredded coconut in a pie pan under the broiler for just a couple of minutes, watching closely and stirring occasionally, until golden brown, and sprinkle over top of pie.

Lemon Cream Cheese Pie

2014 National blue ribbon winner

Makes one 11-inch pie

1 Baked Single Crust (page 3)

8 ounces cream cheese, softened

2 cups powdered sugar

1 (16-ounce) container frozen whipped topping, thawed and divided

¾ cup granulated sugar

Pinch of salt

6 tablespoons cornstarch

5 large egg yolks

1½ cups lemon juice

1½ cups hot water

With an electric stand mixer, mix cream cheese and powdered sugar until smooth. Fold in half the whipped topping and mix a bit longer. With a rubber spatula, continue mixing by hand.

Spread the filling into the bottom of the baked crust.

In a saucepan over high heat, mix the sugar, salt, and cornstarch. Whisk in egg yolks, lemon juice, and hot water. Cook until thickened and center is boiling. Transfer to a plastic bowl and refrigerate.

When mixture is cooled, mound it over the cream cheese layer.

Top with the rest of the whipped topping or Fresh Whipped Cream (page 17). Keep refrigerated.

Raspberry Cream Cheese Pie

2012 National blue ribbon winner

Makes one 11-inch pie

Tip:

While in most cases fresh fruit is best, we suggest using frozen berries or firm store-bought berries for this recipe. The pie will keep much better.

1 Graham Cracker Crust (page 4)

4 ounces cream cheese, softened

1 cup powdered sugar

1 (8-ounce) container frozen whipped topping, thawed and divided

Strawberry/Raspberry Glaze

3¾ cups water

2¼ cups granulated sugar

7 tablespoons (3-ounce box) raspberry gelatin powder

7 tablespoons (3-ounce box) strawberry gelatin powder

6 tablespoons cornstarch

3 tablespoons cold water

6 cups raspberries

Whip the cream cheese at medium speed using an electric stand mixer. Add powdered sugar and continue mixing until smooth. Increase speed to high and whip until light and fluffy.

Add half the whipped topping and mix at a slower speed, being very careful not to overmix. You can finish mixing by hand.

Spread the mixture in the crust.

To make the glaze, combine the water and the sugar in a saucepan and boil for a few minutes until sugar is dissolved completely. Add the gelatin powders and stir until the mixture boils again.

Dissolve the cornstarch in cold water (start with 3 table-spoons water and add more if necessary to make it smooth). Add it quickly to the above mixture and turn down the heat to simmer, stirring slowly until clear bubbles form, about 5 minutes. Cool until thick, about 30 minutes in the refrigerator.

Placed the cooled glaze in a large bowl and mix until smooth. Fold the raspberries into the glaze, coating all the fruit and trying not to smash the fruit.

Mound the fruit mixture over the cream cheese layer. Refrigerate the pie.

Serve with the rest of the whipped topping or Fresh Whipped Cream (page 17).

Pecan Dream Pie

2005 National blue ribbon winner

Makes one 11-inch pie

1 Baked Single Crust (page 3)

8 ounces cream cheese, softened

2 cups powdered sugar

1 (8-ounce) container frozen whipped topping, thawed

1½ cups packed light brown sugar

½ cup whole milk

3 tablespoons salted butter, melted

4 cups pecans, halved

¾ teaspoon salt

Beat the cream cheese using an electric stand mixer. Add the powdered sugar and mix until smooth.

Fold in the whipped topping and mix a bit longer. Remove from the mixer and continue mixing by hand with a rubber spatula.

Spread the filling in the baked crust.

In a saucepan over medium heat, heat the brown sugar, milk, and butter and bring to a boil, stirring while boiling. Boil for 45 seconds (be careful not to overcook). Remove from heat and add the pecans and salt. Stir together and let stand for 10 minutes.

Pour the pecan mixture over the cream cheese layer, mounding in the center. Keep refrigerated.

Strawberry Cream Cheese Pie

....

2009 National blue ribbon winner

Makes one 11-inch pie

● ● ● ● ● ● ● ● ● ● ● ● ● ●

Tip:
....
While in most cases fresh fruit is best, we suggest using frozen berries or firm store-bought berries for this recipe. The pie will keep much better.

1 Graham Cracker Pie Crust (page 4)

4 ounces cream cheese, softened

1 cup powdered sugar

1 (8-ounce) container frozen whipped topping, thawed and divided

Strawberry/Raspberry Glaze

3¾ cups water

2¼ cups granulated sugar

7 tablespoons (3-ounce box) raspberry gelatin powder

7 tablespoons (3-ounce box) strawberry gelatin powder

6 tablespoons cornstarch

3 tablespoons cold water

6 cups strawberries

Whip the cream cheese at medium speed with an electric stand mixer. Add powdered sugar and continue mixing until smooth. Increase speed to high and whip until light and fluffy.

Add half the whipped topping and mix at a slower speed, being very careful not to overmix. You can finish mixing by hand.

Spread the mixture in the crust.

To make the glaze, combine the water and the sugar in a saucepan and boil for a few minutes until sugar is dissolved completely. Add the gelatin powders and stir until the mixture boils again.

Dissolve the cornstarch in cold water (start with 3 table-spoons water and add more if necessary to make it smooth). Add it quickly to the above mixture and turn down the heat to simmer, stirring slowly until clear bubbles form, about 5 minutes. Cool until thick, about 30 minutes in the refrigerator.

Place the cooled glaze in a large bowl and mix until smooth. Fold the strawberries into the glaze, coating all the fruit and trying not to smash the fruit.

Mound the fruit mixture over the cream cheese layer. Refrigerate the pie.

Serve with the rest of the whipped topping or Fresh Whipped Cream (page 17).

Blueberry Cream Cheese Pie

2006 National blue ribbon winner

Makes one 11-inch pie

1 Graham Cracker Pie Crust (page 4)

4 ounces cream cheese, softened

1 cup powdered sugar

1 (8-ounce) container frozen whipped topping, thawed and divided

Blueberry Juice

6½ tablespoons cornstarch

5 tablespoons cold water

4½ cups blueberries

1½ cups granulated sugar

2½ cups water

5 cups blueberries

Whip the cream cheese with an electric stand mixer at medium speed. Add powdered sugar and continue mixing until smooth. Increase speed to high and whip until light and fluffy.

Mix in half the whipped topping, being very careful not to overmix. You can finish mixing by hand.

Spread the mixture in the crust.

To make the blueberry juice, whisk together the cornstarch and cold water. Combine the mixture with the bluberries, sugar, and water in a saucepan and mix with a rubber spatula so the sugar doesn't stick to the bottom. Heat the mixture to boiling, then lower the heat and simmer for 1 hour. Press the berries in a strainer to get all the juice out. Bring strained juice to a boil, add the cornstarch mixture, and cook until thickened.

Remove from heat, add the blueberries, and mix. Pour the mixture onto a cookie sheet and place in freezer for 20 to 30 minutes, until set.

When the blueberry filling is set, mound it over the cream cheese layer. Top with dollops of the remaining whipped topping and refrigerate.

Pumpkin Cream Cheese Pie

2008 National blue ribbon winner

Makes one 11-inch pie

1 Graham Cracker Pie Crust (page 4)

8 ounces cream cheese, softened

1 cup granulated sugar

1 teaspoon vanilla extract

3 large eggs

Pumpkin Pudding

1 individual envelope Knox unflavored gelatin powder

¼ cup cold water

3 large egg whites

3 large egg yokes

1 cup granulated sugar, divided, plus ¼ teaspoon for garnish (optional)

2 cups canned pumpkin puree

1 teaspoon ground cinnamon, plus ¼ teaspoon for garnish (optional)

¼ teaspoon salt

½ cup whole milk

Frozen whipped topping, thawed, or Fresh Whipped Cream (page 17)

Preheat the oven to 375 degrees.

Using a stand mixer, beat the cream cheese, sugar, and vanilla until smooth. Mix in 3 eggs, 1 at a time, until smooth.

Pour into the crust and bake for 20 to 25 minutes, until golden brown. Let cool completely.

To make the pumpkin pudding, dissolve the gelatin powder in water and refrigerate.

Using a stand mixer, beat the egg whites until almost stiff. Add ½ cup of sugar and beat until stiff.

RECIPE CONTINUES

In a saucepan, mix together the pumpkin puree, the remaining ½ cup of sugar, cinnamon, salt, milk, and egg yolks. Fold the beaten egg whites into the pumpkin mixture. Cook until thick and heated completely through.

Remove from heat and add gelatin, which should now be thick and solid. Allow to cool completely.

Mound the pumpkin filling over the cream cheese layer, leaving a little of the cream cheese showing.

Serve or cover the pumpkin pudding with whipped topping or whipped cream and a dusting of ¼ teaspoon each of sugar and cinnamon combined.

Limon Pie

1 Graham Cracker Pie Crust (page 4)

8 ounces cream cheese, softened

1 cup granulated sugar

¼ cup lemon juice

3 large eggs

Sour Cream Filling

3 cups sour cream

3 large egg yolks

1½ cups granulated sugar

¼ cup all-purpose flour

½ cup lime gelatin powder

1 (8-ounce) container frozen whipped topping, thawed

Yellow and green sanding sugar or lemon and lime zests (optional)

Using an electric stand mixer, beat the cream cheese, then add the sugar and the lemon juice. Mix until smooth, adding the eggs, 1 at a time. The mixture should be thick. Pour the mixture into the crust and bake until golden brown, about 1 hour and 25 minutes. Remove from oven and let cool.

You can make the filling while the crust is baking. In a saucepan, stir together the sour cream and egg yolks, then add the sugar and the flour. Cook on high while stirring continuously with a rubber spatula. Watch closely; it can scorch quickly. Cook until the mixture is so thick that it sticks to the spatula when held upright and barely comes off.

Remove from stove, add gelatin powder, mix well, and refrigerate until cool, approximately 30 minutes.

To assemble, mound the filling over the baked cream cheese layer. Finish with a layer of whipped topping.

If desired, sprinkle with sanding sugar or zests.

Blackberry Cream Cheese Pie

Makes one 11-inch pie

Tip:

While in most cases fresh fruit is best, we suggest using frozen berries or firm store-bought berries for this recipe. The pie will keep much better.

1 Graham Cracker Pie Crust (page 4)

4 ounces cream cheese, softened

1 cup powdered sugar

1 (8-ounce) container frozen whipped topping, thawed and divided

Strawberry/Raspberry Glaze

3¾ cups water

2¼ cups granulated sugar

7 tablespoons (3-ounce box) raspberry gelatin powder

7 tablespoons (3-ounce box) strawberry gelatin powder

6 tablespoons cornstarch

3 tablespoons cold water

6 cups blackberries

Whip the cream cheese at medium speed with an electric stand mixer. Add powdered sugar and continue mixing until smooth. Increase speed to high and whip until light and fluffy.

Add half the whipped topping and mix at a slower speed, being very careful not to overmix. You can finish mixing by hand.

Spread the mixture in the crust.

To make the glaze, combine the water and the sugar in a saucepan and boil for a few minutes until sugar is dissolved completely. Add the gelatin powders and stir until the mixture boils again.

Dissolve the cornstarch in cold water (start with 3 tablespoons water and add more if necessary to make it smooth). Add it quickly to the above mixture and turn down the heat to simmer, stirring slowly until clear bubbles form, about 5 minutes. Cool until thick, about 30 minutes in the refrigerator.

Place the cooled glaze in a large bowl and mix until smooth. Fold the blackberries into the glaze, coating all the fruit and trying not to smash the fruit.

Mound the fruit mixture over the cream cheese layer. Refrigerate the pie.

Serve with the rest of the whipped topping or Fresh Whipped Cream (page 17).

Apple Cream Cheese Pie

2010 National blue ribbon winner

Makes one 11-inch pie

1 Baked Single Crust (page 3)

Topping: Dutch Crumb Topping (page 11)

Apple Filling

10 cups Jonathan (or your favorite variety) apples, peeled, cored, and sliced

1½ cups granulated sugar

1 teaspoon ground cinnamon

¼ cup cornstarch

¼ cup cold water

Cream Cheese Filling

8 ounces cream cheese, softened

2 cups powdered sugar

1 (8-ounce) container frozen whipped topping, thawed

¼ cup caramel topping (found with the ice cream toppings at the grocery store), plus additional for garnish (optional)

To make the apple filling, place apples, sugar, and cinnamon in a saucepan on medium heat and cook, stirring occasionally.

In a small bowl, mix the cornstarch with cold water to make it smooth. When the filling comes to a boil and is soft in the center, thicken it with the cornstarch mixture and cook until the cornstarch is cooked clear. Set aside until cooled completely.

RECIPE CONTINUES

Spread the Dutch Crumb Topping on an ungreased cookie sheet and bake for 10 minutes. Stir it, turn the pan, and bake for an additional 10 minutes, or until golden brown.

To make the cream cheese filling, use the whip attachment of a stand mixer at medium speed to beat the cream cheese and powdered sugar until smooth. Fold in the whipped topping and mix well. Spread the filling in the baked crust.

Drizzle the caramel topping over the cream cheese filling and swirl it into the filling with a knife.

When the fruit filling is cool, mound it on top of the cream cheese filling, then cover completely with the baked Dutch Crumb Topping.

Garnish with additional caramel topping, if desired.

Lingonberry Apple Cream Cheese Pie

2012 National blue ribbon winner

Makes one 11-inch pie

1 Baked Single Crust (page 3)

Topping: Dutch Crumb Topping (page 11)

Cream Cheese Filling

8 ounces cream cheese, softened

2 cups powdered sugar

1 (8-ounce) container frozen whipped topping, thawed

Fruit Filling

2 pounds Jonathan (or your favorite variety) apples, peeled, cored, and sliced

½ pound lingonberries

1½ cups granulated sugar

½ cup light brown sugar

1 teaspoon ground cinnamon

⅓ cup cornstarch

¼ cup cold water

To make the cream cheese filling, use the whip attachement of an electric stand mixer at medium speed to beat the cream cheese and powdered sugar until smooth. Fold in the whipped topping and mix well. Spread the filling in the baked crust.

To make the fruit filling, in a saucepan on the stovetop, stir together the apples, lingonberries, both sugars, and cinnamon and cook on high heat, stirring occasionally, until the fruit is soft and the liquid is clear. Combine the cornstarch and water and add to the fruit mixture to thicken. Refrigerate until completely cooled.

Spread the Dutch Crumb Topping on an ungreased cookie sheet and bake for 10 minutes. Stir it, turn the pan, and bake for an additional 10 minutes, or until golden brown.

When the fruit filling is cool, mound it on top of the cream cheese filling, then cover completely with the baked Dutch Crumb Topping.

SOUR CREAM PIES

Sour Cream Lingonberry Pie

Makes one 11-inch pie

1 Baked Single Crust (page 3)

3½ cups sour cream

4 large egg yolks

2 cups granulated sugar

⅓ heaping cup all-purpose flour

⅓ cup black cherry gelatin powder or 1 (3.4-ounce) box black cherry Jell-O powder

⅓ cup raspberry gelatin powder

4½ cups lingonberries

Frozen whipped topping, thawed, or Fresh Whipped Cream (page 17) for serving

Mix the sour cream and egg yolks in a large saucepan. Add the sugar and flour. Cook on high heat, stirring constantly with a rubber spatula. You need to watch very closely; it can scorch quickly. Cook until very thick. When you hold up the spatula, the mixture should stick and barely come off the spatula.

Remove from heat, add the gelatin or Jell-O powders, and mix well. Add the lingonberries and mix together gently.

Pour the mixture into the baked crust. Refrigerate the pie.

Serve with whipped topping or whipped cream.

Tips:

Northwest Wildfoods (www.nwwildfoods.com) will ship frozen lingonberries to your door. The berries are great—no additives, no sugar.

Lingonberries are to Scandinavians what blackberries are to Americans—an abundant wild fruit free for the taking to anyone with a basket, a harvesting fork, and the patience to pick through and clean their harvest. Produced by low, evergreen shrubs throughout Scandinavia's forests, the tart red berries are much smaller and juicier than their distant cousin, the cranberry. Bursting with natural preservatives and pectin, lingonberries were invaluable to earlier generations of Scandinavians.

Sour Cream Raspberry Pie

Makes one 11-inch pie

Tip:

While in most cases fresh fruit is best, we suggest using frozen berries or firm store-bought berries for this recipe. The pie will keep much better.

1 Baked Single Crust (page 3)

3½ cups sour cream

4 large egg yolks

2 cups granulated sugar

⅓ heaping cup all-purpose flour

⅔ cup raspberry gelatin powder

6 cups raspberries

Frozen whipped topping, thawed, or Fresh Whipped Cream (page 17) for serving

Mix the sour cream and egg yolks in a large saucepan. Add the sugar and flour. Cook on high heat, stirring constantly with a rubber spatula. You need to watch very closely; it can scorch quickly. Cook until very thick. When you hold up the spatula, the mixture should stick and barely come off the spatula.

Remove from heat, add the gelatin powder, and mix well. Add the raspberries and mix together gently. Pour the mixture into the baked crust. Refrigerate the pie.

Serve with whipped topping or whipped cream.

Sour Cream Strawberry Pie

Makes one 11-inch pie

Tip:

While in most cases fresh fruit is best, we suggest using frozen berries or firm store-bought berries for this recipe. The pie will keep much better.

1 Baked Single Crust (page 3)

3½ cups sour cream

4 large egg yolks

2 cups granulated sugar

⅓ heaping cup all-purpose flour

⅔ cup strawberry gelatin powder

6 cups strawberries, quartered

Frozen whipped topping, thawed, or Fresh Whipped Cream (page 17) for serving

Mix the sour cream and egg yolks in a large saucepan. Add the sugar and flour. Cook on high heat, stirring constantly with a rubber spatula. You need to watch very closely; it can scorch quickly. Cook until very thick. When you hold up the spatula, the mixture should stick and barely come off the spatula.

Remove from heat, add the gelatin powder, and mix well. Add the strawberries and mix together gently. Pour the mixture into the baked crust. Refrigerate the pie.

Serve with whipped topping or whipped cream.

Sour Cream Blackberry Pie

Makes one 11-inch pie

Tip:

While in most cases fresh fruit is best, we suggest using frozen berries or firm store-bought berries for this recipe. The pie will keep much better.

1 Baked Single Crust (page 3)

3½ cups sour cream

4 large egg yolks

2 cups granulated sugar

⅓ heaping cup all-purpose flour

⅔ cup black cherry gelatin powder, or 2 (3.4-ounce) boxes black cherry Jell-O powder

6 cups blackberries

Frozen whipped topping, thawed, or Fresh Whipped Cream (page 17) for serving

Mix the sour cream and egg yolks in a large saucepan. Add the sugar and flour. Cook on high heat, stirring constantly with a rubber spatula. You need to watch very closely; it can scorch quickly. Cook until very thick. When you hold up the spatula, the mixture should stick and barely come off the spatula.

Remove from heat, add the gelatin or Jell-O powder, and mix well. Add the blackberries and mix together gently. Pour the mixture into the baked crust. Refrigerate the pie.

Serve with whipped topping or whipped cream.

Raspberry White Chocolate Pie

2008 National blue ribbon winner

Makes one 11-inch pie

1 Baked Single Crust (page 3)

1 (12-ounce) bag white chocolate chips, divided
2 (8-ounce) containers frozen whipped topping, thawed
2½ cups sour cream
4 cups raspberries
½ cup mini semisweet chocolate chips
1 tablespoon salted butter, melted

Place half the white chocolate chips in a plastic cup and microwave in 30-second intervals, stirring between intervals until fully melted. Spread the melted chocolate evenly on the bottom of the baked crust.

To make the filling, in a saucepan over low heat, melt the remaining chocolate chips and stir together with 1 container of whipped topping. Refrigerate until thick.

When cooled and thick, transfer the chocolate mixture to a large bowl, add the sour cream, and mix well. Lightly fold in the other container of whipped topping.

Spread a small amount of filling in the crust. Add 2 cups of raspberries, avoiding the sides of the crust and keeping the raspberries in the center of the filling.

Add about half the remaining filling, covering all the raspberries. Add the rest of the raspberries (except for 8), still not touching the crust. Finish with the rest of the filling and smooth with a rubber spatula. Arrange 8 raspberries around the top of the pie.

In a microwave, melt the mini chocolate chips with the butter, stir, and drizzle over the top of the pie with a crisscross pattern. Refrigerate the pie.

Strawberry White Chocolate Pie

2012 National blue ribbon winner

Makes one 11-inch pie

1 Baked Single Crust (page 3)

1 (12-ounce) bag white chocolate chips, divided

2 (8-ounce) cartons frozen whipped topping, thawed

2½ cups sour cream

Red food coloring

4 cups strawberries, chopped

4 whole strawberries, halved

½ cup mini semisweet chocolate chips

1 tablespoon salted butter, melted

Place half the white chocolate chips in a plastic cup and microwave in 30-second intervals, stirring between intervals until fully melted. Spread the melted chocolate evenly on the bottom of the baked crust.

To make the filling, in a saucepan over low heat, melt the remaining chocolate chips and stir together with 1 container of whipped topping. Refrigerate until thick.

When cooled and thick, transfer the chocolate mixture to a large bowl, add the sour cream, and mix well. Lightly fold in the other container of whipped topping. Add 1 or 2 drops of food coloring and mix until you have a nice pink color.

Spread a small amount of filling in the crust. Add 2 cups of chopped strawberries, avoiding the sides of the crust and keeping the strawberries in the center of the filling.

Add about half the remaining filling, covering all the strawberries. Add the rest of the chopped strawberries, still not touching the crust. Finish with the rest of the filling and smooth with a rubber spatula. Arrange the halved strawberries around the top of the pie.

In a microwave, melt the mini chocolate chips with the butter, stir, and drizzle over the top of the pie with a crisscross pattern. Refrigerate the pie.

Sour Cream Apple Blueberry Pie

Makes one 11-inch pie

Tip:

While in most cases fresh fruit is best, we suggest using frozen berries or firm store-bought berries for this recipe. The pie will keep much better.

1 Baked Single Crust (page 3)

3½ cups sour cream

4 large egg yolks

2 cups granulated sugar

⅔ heaping cup all-purpose flour

3 cups Jonathan (or your favorite variety) apples, peeled, cored, and sliced

4½ cups blueberries

Frozen whipped topping, thawed, or Fresh Whipped Cream (page 17) for serving

Mix the sour cream and egg yolks in a large saucepan. Add the sugar, flour, and apples. Cook on high heat, stirring constantly with a rubber spatula. You need to watch very closely; it can scorch quickly. Cook until very thick. When you hold up the spatula, the mixture should stick and barely come off the spatula.

Remove from heat, add the blueberries, and mix together gently. Pour the mixture into the baked crust. Refrigerate the pie.

Serve with whipped topping or whipped cream.

Sour Cream Peach Pie

....

Makes one 11-inch pie

● ● ● ● ● ● ● ● ● ● ● ● ● ●

Tip:

....

While in most cases fresh fruit is best, we suggest using frozen berries or firm store-bought berries for this recipe. The pie will keep much better.

1 Baked Single Crust (page 3)

3½ cups sour cream

4 large egg yolks

2 cups granulated sugar

⅓ heaping cup all-purpose flour

⅔ cup peach gelatin powder

4½ cups peaches, diced

Frozen whipped topping, thawed, or Fresh Whipped Cream (page 17) for serving

Mix the sour cream and egg yolks in a large saucepan. Add the sugar and flour. Cook on high heat, stirring constantly with a rubber spatula. You need to watch very closely; it can scorch quickly. Cook until very thick. When you hold up the spatula, the mixture should stick and barely come off the spatula.

Remove from heat, add the gelatin powder, and mix well. Add the peaches and mix together gently. Pour into the baked crust. Refrigerate the pie.

Serve with whipped topping or whipped cream.

MERINGUE PIES

With all the hard work we put into making the large volume of pies at Norske Nook each day, sometimes we like to lighten the mood and add some fun and excitement. They call me the joker, and I do love a good practical joke now and then. One time while Shari Brown was mixing pie dough, I snuck in a large rubber cockroach and put it under a dough ball so that when she flipped the dough over to knead it, she would find the cockroach. It took only a few seconds before the screaming and jumping started!

But Shari got me back for that one. She was baking meringues in the oven, but the pilot light kept going out, so I replaced the pilot sensor. A few days later, she was baking meringues again, and I was planning to make rosettes in the donut fryer, except that pilot light kept going out. Shari told me she was still having problems with the pilot light I had just replaced, so I was bent down trying to light the pilot lights when Shari snuck up behind me with a large air-filled paper bag and popped the bag—BOOM! I immediately dropped to the floor to roll because I was sure I was on fire! All the bakers and coworkers got a good laugh. That's my meringue story, and I'm sticking to it!

—Jerry Bechard

Meringue

Makes one 11-inch pie

1 Baked Single Crust (page 3)

15 large egg whites

¼ heaping teaspoon cream of tartar

2 cups powdered sugar

Tips:

Be sure the bowls are completely clean, without a speck of grease or residue in the bowl or on the mixer.

Be sure no egg yolks get into the egg whites.

To ensure a nice firm texture, don't beat the whites too long before adding the powdered sugar.

Preheat the oven to 400 degrees.

Using an electric mixer on high speed, beat the egg whites and cream of tartar in a medium bowl until foamy. Gradually add the sugar, beating until soft peaks form.

With a rubber spatula, spread the meringue evenly (don't dump it all in at once) over a cooled pie filling, sealing to the edges of the crust.

Bake 15 to 20 minutes, until meringue is golden brown. Cool completely on a wire rack. Keep the pie refrigerated.

Coconut Meringue Pie

Makes one 11-inch pie

1 Baked Single Crust (page 3)

1 batch of Vanilla Pudding (page 17), cooled

1 batch of Meringue (page 114)

2 cups shredded or flaked sweetened coconut, plus a little extra to sprinkle on top

Preheat the oven to 375 degrees.

In a saucepan, prepare the pudding. After it has thickened and is still on the stove, add the coconut and cook for a minute. Remove from heat and cool slightly.

Pour the mixture into the baked crust, top with the meringue, and sprinkle the meringue with coconut. Bake for about 20 minutes, until golden brown. Cool completely on a wire rack. Keep the pie refrigerated.

Rhubarb Cream Meringue Pie

Makes one 11-inch pie

1 Baked Single Crust (page 3)

1 batch of Meringue (page 114)

½ cup (1 stick) salted butter
6 cups rhubarb
2 cups granulated sugar, divided
3 large egg yolks
½ cup all-purpose flour
½ cup half-and-half

Preheat the oven to 375 degrees.

In a large saucepan, melt the butter on low heat. Add the rhubarb and cook until the rhubarb is coated with butter. Add 1½ cups sugar and cook until rhubarb is soft.

Mix the egg yolks, ½ cup sugar, flour, and half-and-half in a medium bowl until smooth. Add this mixture to the hot rhubarb mixture. Cook until thick.

Remove from heat and pour into the baked crust. Refrigerate until cooled.

Top with the meringue and bake for 15 to 20 minutes, until golden brown. Cool completely on a wire rack. Keep the pie refrigerated.

Lemon Meringue Pie

Makes one 11-inch pie

1 Baked Single Crust (page 3)

1 batch of Lemon Pudding (page 15), cooled

1 batch of Meringue (page 114)

Preheat the oven to 375 degrees.

In a saucepan, prepare the pudding and cool.

Pour the cooled pudding into the baked crust, top with the meringue, and bake for 20 minutes, until golden brown. Cool completely on a wire rack. Keep the pie refrigerated.

Sour Cream Raisin Meringue Pie

2012 National blue ribbon winner

Makes one 11-inch pie

1 Baked Single Crust (page 3)

1 batch of Meringue (page 114)

3½ cups sour cream

4 large egg yolks

2 cups granulated sugar

⅓ heaping cup all-purpose flour

2 cups raisins

Preheat the oven to 375 degrees.

In a saucepan, stir together the sour cream and egg yolks. Add the sugar, flour, and raisins. Cook on high heat, stirring constantly with a rubber spatula. You need to watch very closely; it can scorch quickly. Cook until very thick. When you hold the spatula up out of the pan, the mixture should stick and barely come off the spatula.

Remove from heat and pour into the baked crust. Refrigerate until cooled.

Top with the meringue and bake for 15 to 20 minutes, until golden brown. Cool completely on a wire rack. Keep the pie refrigerated.

SINGLE-CRUST PIES

Pecan Fudge Pie

2013 National blue ribbon winner

Makes one 11-inch pie

1 Unbaked Single Crust (page 2)

5 large eggs

1 cup granulated sugar

¾ cup (1½ sticks) salted butter, melted

1¾ cups Karo syrup

1 cup chocolate chips

2 cups pecans, halved

Preheat the oven to 375 degrees.

Combine the eggs, sugar, and butter in a bowl. Whisk until the eggs are broken up, being careful not to overmix. Mix in the syrup with a rubber spatula.

Pour the mixture into the crust.

Sprinkle the chocolate chips over the filling and then swirl them in. Sprinkle the pecans over the entire pie, starting around the edges and then filling in the center.

Bake until golden brown, about 1 hour and 25 minutes.

Custard Pie

2006 National blue ribbon winner

Makes one 11-inch pie

Tip:

To help prevent spilling, place the pie crust on the oven rack before filling it with the mixture.

—*Heidi Myren-Becker, general manager of the Osseo Norske Nook*

1 Unbaked Single Crust (page 2)

14 large egg yolks

2 large whole eggs

1 cup granulated sugar

1 tablespoon vanilla extract

Pinch of salt

3 cups whole milk

Ground nutmeg to sprinkle

Preheat the oven to 375 degrees.

In a large bowl, whisk together the egg yolks, whole eggs, sugar, vanilla, and salt. Add milk and mix well.

Pour the mixture into the crust. Sprinkle with nutmeg.

Bake until set, about 45 minutes. Check doneness with a toothpick.

Lemon Poppy Seed Pie

Makes one 11-inch pie

1 Graham Cracker Pie Crust (page 4)

2 (14-ounce) cans sweetened condensed milk

⅔ cup lemonade concentrate

2 (16-ounce) containers frozen whipped topping, thawed

3 tablespoons poppy seeds

Yellow food coloring

Using an electric stand mixer, mix together the condensed milk and lemonade concentrate until smooth and thickened. Fold in the whipped topping.

Spread half the mixture in the crust.

Add 3 tablespoons poppy seeds and 6 drops of food coloring to the rest of the mixture. Mix well and spoon over the first layer.

Refrigerate the pie.

Raisin Bread Pudding Pie with Vanilla Sauce

2010 National blue ribbon winner

Makes one 11-inch pie

● ● ● ● ● ● ● ● ● ● ● ●

1 Unbaked Single Crust (page 2)

5 large eggs

¾ cup granulated sugar

2 teaspoons vanilla extract

½ teaspoon salt

1 teaspoon ground cinnamon

½ cup raisins

1 (20-ounce) can crushed pineapple, drained

¼ cup (½ stick) salted butter, melted

3 cups hot whole milk

1½ cups Jonathan (or your favorite variety) apples, peeled, cored, and diced

1 loaf sliced raisin bread, cubed (The night before you make this pie, lay out the slices on a sheet pan. The next day cut off the crusts and cube the slices into 1-inch pieces.)

Vanilla Sauce

½ cup granulated sugar

1 tablespoon cornstarch

1 cup boiling water

2 tablespoons salted butter

1 teaspoon vanilla extract

¼ teaspoon salt

Preheat the oven to 375 degrees.

In a large bowl, whisk together all the ingredients except the bread and the apples. Add the bread cubes and the apples and let it soak for 2 to 3 minutes.

Mound the mixture into the crust.

Put aluminum foil under the pie pan and also cover the top with aluminum foil.

Place the pie in a shallow pan with an inch of water.

Bake for about 2 hours. Uncover the pie for the last 15 minutes of baking.

To make the sauce, combine the sugar and cornstarch in a saucepan. Add the boiling water and boil for 5 minutes, stirring constantly. Remove from the heat and mix in the butter, vanilla, and salt.

Cover the pie with the sauce.

This pie could also be served with warm rum sauce (page 42).

Pecan Stout Pie

2010 National blue ribbon winner

Makes one 11-inch pie

1 Unbaked Single Crust (page 2)

5 large eggs

1 cup granulated sugar

¼ cup malted milk powder

⅓ cup stout beer

¾ cup (1½ sticks) salted butter, melted

1¾ cups Karo syrup

2 cups pecans, halved

Preheat the oven to 375 degrees.

Combine the eggs, sugar, malted milk powder, beer, and butter in a bowl. Whisk until the eggs are broken up, being careful not to overmix. Mix in the syrup with a rubber spatula.

Pour the mixture into the crust.

Sprinkle the pecans over the entire pie, starting around the edges and then filling in the center.

Bake until golden brown, about 1 hour and 25 minutes.

Pecan Pie

Makes one 11-inch pie

1 Unbaked Single Crust (page 2)

5 large eggs

1 cup granulated sugar

¾ cup (1½ sticks) salted butter, melted

1¾ cups Karo syrup

2 cups pecans, halved

Preheat the oven to 350 degrees.

Combine the eggs, sugar, and butter in a bowl. Whisk until the eggs are broken up, being careful not to overmix. Mix in the Karo syrup with a rubber spatula.

Pour the mixture into the crust.

Sprinkle the pecans over the entire pie, starting around the edges and then filling in the center.

Bake until golden brown, about 1 hour and 25 minutes.

Pumpkin Pie

Makes one 11-inch pie

1 Unbaked Single Crust (page 2)

2¾ cups pumpkin puree

1 cup granulated sugar

1 cup light brown sugar

4 large eggs

1 tablespoon pumpkin pie spice

½ teaspoon salt

1¾ cups whole milk

Preheat the oven to 375 degrees.

In a large bowl, whisk together all the ingredients except the milk, then add the milk and whisk again.

Pour the mixture into the crust.

Bake for 45 minutes to 1 hour, or until a knife inserted in the center is clean.

STIRRED PUDDING PIES

Jerry, Flicka, and Butterscotch Pie
· ·

Growing up we almost always had dessert after our meals, ranging from cookies to cakes to pies. One of my all-time favorites was Helen's butterscotch pie. Whenever I stopped to check on our Norske Nook in Hayward, I would have my dear friend and manager of this location, Flicka Torpen, cut us both a slice, because she loved butterscotch pie too.

—Jerry Bechard

Butterscotch Pie

Makes one 11-inch pie

1 Baked Single Crust (page 3)

2 cups packed light brown sugar

3 tablespoons all-purpose flour

3 tablespoons cornstarch

3 large egg yolks

3 cups whole milk

⅓ cup salted butter, melted

1 teaspoon maple flavoring

1 (8-ounce) container frozen whipped topping, thawed

½ cup pecans, chopped

Pack the brown sugar very well and level the tablespoons of flour and cornstarch. Put them all in a saucepan and mix well. Whisk in the egg yolks and milk. Add the butter and cook over high heat, stirring continuously. Cook until the mixture thickens and boils in the center. Remove from heat and stir in the maple flavoring.

Pour into the baked crust. Cover the pie with plastic wrap and refrigerate until ready to serve.

Top with whipped topping all the way to the edges. Garnish with pecans.

Banana Cream Pie

2003 National blue ribbon winner

Makes one 11-inch pie

1 Graham Cracker Pie Crust (page 4)

1 batch of Vanilla Pudding (page17), cooled

5 to 7 bananas, sliced

Frozen whipped topping, thawed, or Fresh Whipped Cream (page 17) for serving (optional)

Spread a small amount of the cooled vanilla pudding evenly over the bottom of the crust.

Add a layer of bananas, then the remainder of the pudding, being sure to cover the bananas completely, or they will turn dark. No bananas should show through.

Cover the pie with plastic wrap and refrigerate until ready to serve.

Serve with whipped topping or whipped cream, if desired.

Chocolate Cream Pie

....

● ● ● ● ● ● ● ● ● ● ● ● ●

1 Baked Single Crust (page 3)

1 batch of Chocolate Pudding (page 16), cooled

Frozen whipped topping, thawed, or Fresh Whipped Cream (page 17) for serving
½ **cup chocolate chips**

Pour the cooled chocolate pudding into the cooled pie crust.

Cover the pie with plastic wrap and refrigerate until ready to serve.

Serve with whipped topping or whipped cream, then sprinkle with chocolate chips.

FROZEN PIES

Cookies and Cream Pie

2012 National blue ribbon winner

Makes one 11-inch pie

1 Oreo Cookie Pie Crust (page 4)

3 cups heavy whipping cream

1⅓ cups powdered sugar

1 teaspoon vanilla extract

1 (8-ounce) container frozen whipped topping, thawed, plus additional for garnish

3 cups crushed Oreo cookies, divided

Using a stand mixer on low speed, mix the cream, sugar, and vanilla. Gradually increase the speed until the mixture is thick. Be careful not to overmix.

Fold the whipped topping into mixture with a rubber spatula, then add all but about ¼ cup of the crushed Oreos.

Mound the mixture into the crust and sprinkle the rest of the crushed Oreos on top. Freeze the pie.

Serve with whipped topping garnished along the edges.

Butterscotch Mousse Pie

Makes one 11-inch pie

1 Baked Single Crust (page 3)

4 cups (1 quart) heavy whipping cream

1⅔ cups powdered sugar

1 teaspoon vanilla extract

½ cup cook-and-serve butterscotch pudding powder

2 (8-ounce) containers frozen whipped topping, thawed (one for filling and one for garnish)

Using a stand mixer on low speed, mix the cream, sugar, vanilla, and pudding powder. Gradually increase the speed until the mixture is thick. Be careful not to overmix.

Fold 1 container of whipped topping into the mixture with a rubber spatula.

Mound the mixture into the crust. Freeze the pie.

Serve with whipped topping garnished along the edges.

Northwoods Root Beer Float Pie

2008 National blue ribbon winner

Makes one 11-inch pie

1 Baked Single Crust (page 3)

4 cups heavy whipping cream

1⅔ cups powdered sugar

⅓ cup root beer syrup

½ cup cook-and-serve vanilla pudding powder

2 (8-ounce) containers frozen whipped topping, thawed (one for filling and one for topping)

With a stand electric mixer at low speed, mix the cream and sugar. Add the syrup and pudding powder and gradually increase the speed until the mixture is thick. Be careful not to overmix.

Fold 1 container of whipped topping into the mixture with a rubber spatula.

Mound the mixture into the crust. Freeze the pie.

Serve with whipped topping garnished along the edges.

Holiday Mint Pie

1 Baked Single Crust (page 3)

1 cup sour cream

8 ounces cream cheese, softened

1 cup powdered sugar

3 cups heavy whipping cream

⅓ cup cook-and-serve vanilla pudding powder

Green food coloring

1 cup crushed peppermint candies (reserve 2 tablespoons for garnish)

Frozen whipped topping, thawed, or Fresh Whipped Cream (page 17) for serving

In a large mixing bowl, combine the sour cream, cream cheese, and sugar. Mix well until smooth.

In a separate bowl and using a stand mixer on low speed, combine the whipping cream, pudding powder, and 1 drop of food coloring. Gradually increase speed until the mixture is thick.

Fold the candies into the cream cheese mixture.

Fold the whipping cream mixture into the cream cheese mixture.

Mound the mixture into the crust.

Sprinkle crushed peppermint candies in the center. Freeze the pie.

Serve with whipped topping garnished along the edges.

Amaretto Fudge Pie

Makes one 11-inch pie

1 Baked Single Crust (page 3)

2 individual envelopes Knox unflavored gelatin powder

½ cup amaretto liqueur

4 cups heavy whipping cream

1⅔ cups powdered sugar

1 tablespoon vanilla extract

2 tablespoons cocoa powder

½ cup cook-and-serve chocolate pudding powder

1 (8-ounce) container frozen whipped topping, thawed, plus additional for garnish (optional)

½ cup pecans, chopped

Dissolve the unflavored gelatin powder in the amaretto. Refrigerate to set.

Using a stand mixer on low speed, mix the cream, sugar, vanilla, and cocoa and pudding powders. Gradually increase the speed until the mixture thickens. Be careful not to overmix.

With a long-handled spatula, fold in the topping, pecans, and cooled gelatin.

Mound the mixture into the crust. Freeze the pie.

Serve with more whipped topping or Fresh Whipped Cream (page 17), if desired.

Orange Dream Pie

2012 National blue ribbon winner

Makes one 11-inch pie

1 Baked Single Crust (page 3) or 1 Oreo Cookie Pie Crust (page 4)

4 cups heavy whipping cream

1⅔ cups powdered sugar

¾ cup cook-and-serve vanilla pudding powder

1 (8-ounce) container frozen whipped topping, thawed

½ cup orange gelatin powder

Using a stand mixer on low speed, mix the cream, sugar, and pudding powder. Gradually increase the speed until the mixture is thick. Be careful not to overmix.

Fold about ¾ of the whipped topping into the mixture with a rubber spatula.

Take out 3 cups of the mixture and set aside. Add the gelatin powder to the rest of the mixture and stir. Swirl the two mixtures together and mound into the crust. Freeze the pie.

Serve with whipped topping garnished along the edges.

Chocolate Mousse Pie

· ·

2013 National blue ribbon winner

Makes one 11-inch pie

· · · · · · · · · · · · · ·

1 Chocolate Lined Pastry Crust (page 3)

4 cups (1 quart) heavy whipping cream

1⅔ cups powdered sugar

1 tablespoon vanilla extract

2 tablespoons cocoa powder

½ cup cook-and-serve chocolate pudding powder

1 (8-ounce) container frozen whipped topping, thawed, plus additional for garnish

2 tablespoons chocolate syrup

Using a stand mixer, mix the cream, sugar, vanilla, and cocoa and pudding powders on low speed. Gradually increase the speed until the mixture is thick. Be careful not to overmix.

Fold the whipped topping into the mixture with a rubber spatula.

Mound the mixture into the crust and gently swirl in chocolate syrup. Freeze the pie.

Serve with whipped topping garnished along the edges.

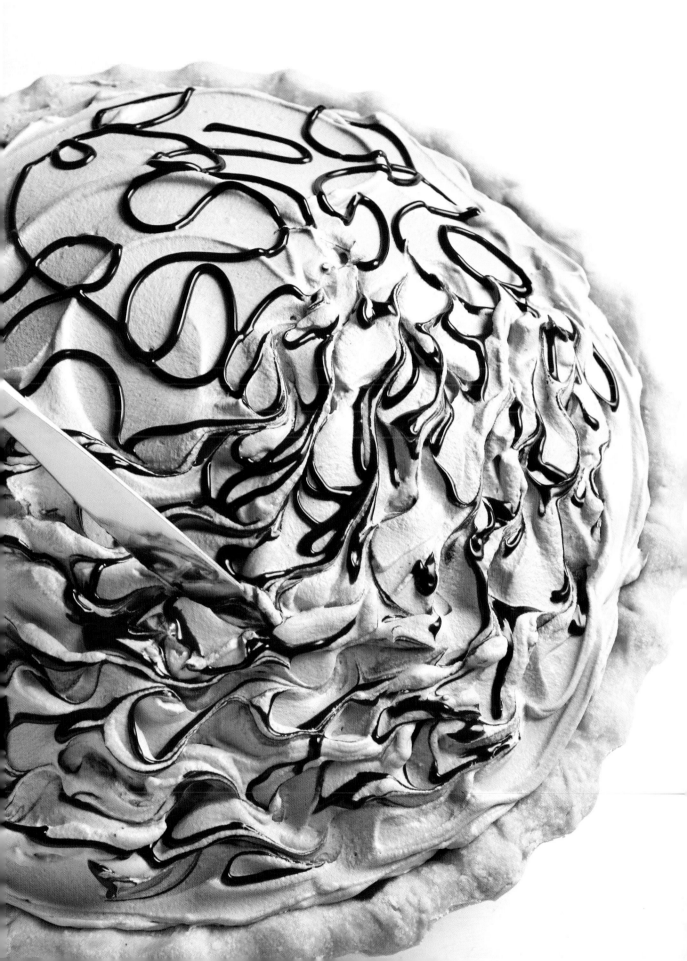

SUGAR-FREE PIES

Sugar-Free Rhubarb Pie

Makes one 11-inch pie

1 Double Crust (page 3)

¾ cup Equal brand sweetener

2 tablespoons minute tapioca

3 large eggs

Pinch of ground nutmeg

2½ pounds rhubarb, cut into ¾-inch pieces

1 tablespoon cold salted butter, cut into 3 slices

3 tablespoons half-and-half

Preheat the oven to 375 degrees.

Using a stand mixer, mix the sweetener, tapioca, eggs, and nutmeg. Fold in the rhubarb until it is well coated.

Pour the mixture into the crust and dot with the butter slices. It will seem like a heaping pie, but the rhubarb will shrink a lot when cooked.

Cover the pie with the remaining crust, crimp around the rim, and cut slits in the top. Sprinkle with half-and-half.

Bake until the rhubarb is bubbling and soft in the center (a knife comes out clear), about 2 hours. Frozen rhubarb will take longer to bake than fresh.

Sugar-Free Apple Pie

Makes one 11-inch pie

1 Double Crust (page 3)

2½ pounds Jonathan (or your favorite variety) apples, peeled, cored, and sliced

¾ cup Equal brand sweetener

2 tablespoons minute tapioca

1 teaspoon ground cinnamon

Pinch of ground nutmeg

1 tablespoon cold salted butter, cut into 3 slices

1 tablespoon half-and-half

Preheat the oven to 375 degrees.

Place about half the apples in the crust.

Combine the Equal, tapioca, cinnamon, and nutmeg. Sprinkle half the dry mixture over the apples. Add the remaining apples, followed by the remaining dry mixture. Dot with the butter slices.

Cover the pie with the remaining crust, crimp around the rim, and cut slits in the top. Sprinkle with half-and-half.

Bake until the apples are bubbling and soft in the center (a knife comes out clear), about 2 hours.

Sugar-Free Blueberry, Cherry, and Peach Pie

2008 National blue ribbon winner

Makes one 11-inch pie

● ● ● ● ● ● ● ● ● ● ● ●

1 **Double Crust (page 3)**

2½ pounds **fruit—blueberries, cherries, and peaches**

¾ cup **Equal brand sweetener**

2 tablespoons **minute tapioca**

1 tablespoon **cold salted butter, cut into 3 slices**

1 tablespoon **half-and-half**

Preheat the oven to 375 degrees.

Place about half the fruit in the crust.

Combine the Equal and tapioca. Sprinkle half the dry mixture over the fruit. Add the remaining fruit, followed by the remaining dry mixture. Dot with the butter slices.

Cover with the remaining crust, crimp around the rim, and cut slits in the top. Sprinkle with half-and-half.

Bake until the fruit is bubbling and soft in the center (a knife comes out clear), about 2 hours.

CHEESECAKES

A Story of My Sister Anita's Cheesecakes

My sister Anita absolutely loved to cook and bake, and when she heard about me purchasing the Norske Nook restaurant, she immediately went to work experimenting with cheesecakes. I was already hooked on her plain New York–style cheesecake, but I was excited to try her new variations and serve them at Norske Nook.

Anita was a biology major and a substitute teacher at my grade school. She had such a wonderful way of teaching children and adults about nature. One of my fondest memories is picking berries with her in Oregon. She explained every plant species on the hillside overlooking the Pacific Ocean, and then we filled our buckets with berries. Later she made a blackberry cheesecake that was to die for!

—Jerry Bechard

Norske Nook Cheesecake

Makes two 9-inch round cheesecakes

2 Graham Cracker Cheesecake Crusts (page 6)

1 cup heavy whipping cream

¼ cup powdered sugar

2 teaspoons vanilla extract, divided

3 pounds cream cheese, softened

2 cups granulated sugar

8 large eggs

½ cup all-purpose flour

Sour Cream Topping

1 cup sour cream

3 tablespoons granulated sugar

1 teaspoon vanilla extract

Preheat the oven to 300 degrees.

Using an electric mixer at low speed and gradually increasing speed, combine the cream, powdered sugar, and 1 teaspoon vanilla in a medium bowl. Mix until stiff and set aside.

In a separate bowl, mix at low to medium speed the cream cheese and granulated sugar. Add the eggs and 1 teaspoon vanilla. Mix, then scrape down the sides and bottom of the bowl with a rubber spatula. Add the flour and mix well.

Fold in the stiffened cream mixture from the first bowl, and mix until smooth. Pour the mixture into the crusts.

Bake at 300 degrees for 30 minutes, then decrease the oven temperature to 170 degrees and bake for an additional 80 minutes.

While the cheesecakes are baking, you can make the topping. Mix together the sour cream, sugar, and vanilla extract.

When the cheesecakes are done baking, remove them from the oven and increase the temperature to 300 degrees. Very carefully and evenly spread the topping over the cheesecakes. Return them to the oven for an additional 30 minutes. They are done when the middle does not wiggle and shake. Observe very closely when deciding doneness. Remove from oven and cool. You can leave them plain or top them with Lingonberry Topping (page 19) or Blueberry Topping (page 12).

Chocolate Caramel Cheesecake

....

Makes two 9-inch round cheesecakes

. . . .

2 Oreo Cookie Cheesecake Crusts (page 7)

1 cup heavy whipping cream

¼ cup powdered sugar

2 teaspoons vanilla extract, divided

3 pounds cream cheese, softened

2 cups granulated sugar

8 large eggs

½ cup all-purpose flour

2 cups mini chocolate chips

Caramel topping (found with the ice cream toppings at the grocery store) for drizzling

Preheat the oven to 300 degrees.

Using an electric mixer at low speed and gradually increasing speed, combine the cream, powdered sugar, and 1 teaspoon vanilla in a medium bowl. Mix until stiff and set aside.

In a separate bowl, mix at low to medium speed the cream cheese and granulated sugar. Add the eggs and 1 teaspoon vanilla. Mix, then scrape down the sides and bottom of the bowl with a rubber spatula. Add the flour and mix well.

Fold in the stiffened cream mixture from the first bowl, and mix until smooth. Pour the mixture into the crusts. Sprinkle with chocolate chips and drizzle on caramel topping. Gently swirl chips and caramel with knife.

Bake at 300 degrees for 30 minutes, then decrease the oven temperature to 170 degrees and bake for an additional 80 minutes. Check and bake until set, up to 20 to 30 more minutes. You can tell doneness when the middle does not wiggle or shake. Observe very closely when deciding doneness. Remove from oven and cool.

Pumpkin Cheesecake

Makes two 9-inch round cheesecakes

• • • • • • • • • • • • • • •

2 Graham Cracker Cheesecake Crusts (page 6)

½ cup heavy whipping cream

2 cups canned pumpkin puree

2 cups granulated sugar

3 pounds cream cheese, softened

6 large eggs

1⅓ tablespoon pumpkin pie spice

1 teaspoon salt

Frozen whipped topping, thawed, or Fresh Whipped Cream (page 17) for serving (optional)

Candy corn for serving (optional)

Preheat the oven to 300 degrees.

In a small bowl, mix at low to medium speed the cream until stiff, then set aside. Using an electric mixer at medium speed, mix together the pumpkin puree, sugar, and cream cheese. Add the eggs, pumpkin pie spice, and salt. Mix, then scrape down the sides of the mixing bowl with a rubber spatula. Fold in the cream until smooth. Pour the mixture into the crusts.

Bake at 300 degrees for 30 to 40 minutes, then decrease the oven temperature to 170 degrees and bake for an additional 80 minutes.

You can tell when they are done by making sure the middle does not wiggle and shake. Observe very closely when deciding doneness. Remove from oven and cool.

Top with whipped cream and candy corn for a great fall treat.

TORTES

Strawberry Torte

Makes one 9-by-13-inch torte

1 Graham Cracker Crust for Tortes (page 5)

3¾ cups water

1½ cups strawberry gelatin powder

6 cups strawberries, chopped

1 (8-ounce) container frozen whipped topping, thawed

Boil the water. Add the gelatin powder and stir until completely dissolved. Add the berries and stir. Refrigerate until partially set, approximately 30 minutes.

Spread the cooled mixture over the crust. Cover with plastic wrap and refrigerate until completely set.

Serve with whipped topping.

Blackberry or Raspberry Torte

Makes one 9-by-13-inch torte

1 Graham Cracker Crust for Tortes (page 5)

3½ cups water

1¼ cups raspberry gelatin powder

6 cups blackberries or raspberries (reserve a few for garnish)

1 (8-ounce) container frozen whipped topping, thawed

Boil the water. Combine the water and the gelatin in a bowl and stir until dissolved. Add the berries and stir. Refrigerate until partially set, approximately 30 minutes.

Spread the cooled mixure over the crust. Cover with plastic wrap and refrigerate until completely set.

Serve with whipped topping and berries.

Cherry or Blueberry Torte

Makes one 9-by-13-inch torte

1 Graham Cracker Crust for Tortes (page 5)

1 (1-quart) jar of Norske Nook Cherry or Blueberry Pie Filling

1 (8-ounce) container frozen whipped topping, thawed

Spread the pie filling in the crust. Cover with topping. Refrigerate.

Butterscotch Coconut Torte

1 Nut Crust for Tortes (page 6)

1¼ cups light brown sugar

1½ tablespoons all-purpose flour

1½ tablespoons cornstarch

1½ cups flaked sweetened coconut

1 cup cook-and-serve vanilla pudding powder

2 large egg yolks

3 cups whole milk

1 teaspoon maple flavoring

Cream Cheese Filling

8 ounces cream cheese, softened

2 cups powdered sugar

1 (8-ounce) container frozen whipped topping, thawed

1 (8-ounce) container frozen whipped topping, thawed, or Fresh Whipped Cream (page 17)

In a large saucepan, combine the sugar, flour, cornstarch, coconut, and pudding powder. Add the egg yolks and milk and whisk. Cook over high heat until thick, like a butterscotch pudding. Once thick, add the maple flavoring. Refrigerate to set.

To make the cream cheese filling, mix the cream cheese with the powdered sugar, using an electric stand mixer. Add the whipped topping and mix until well blended and smooth.

Spread the crust with the cream cheese filling, then layer with the butterscotch coconut mixture and top with the whipped cream.

Chocolate Cream Torte

Makes one 9-by-13-inch torte

1 Nut Crust for Tortes (page 6)

1 batch of Chocolate Pudding (page 16), cooled

Cream Cheese Filling

8 ounces cream cheese, softened

2 cups powdered sugar

1 (8-ounce) container frozen whipped topping, thawed

1 (8-ounce) container frozen whipped topping, thawed, or Fresh Whipped Cream (page 17)

1 (12-ounce) bag semisweet mini chocolate chips for garnish

To make the cream cheese filling, mix the cream cheese with the sugar, using an electric stand mixer. Add the topping and mix until well blended and smooth.

Spread the crust with the cream cheese filling, add a layer of the pudding, and top with the whipped topping or whipped cream. Garnish with chocolate chips.

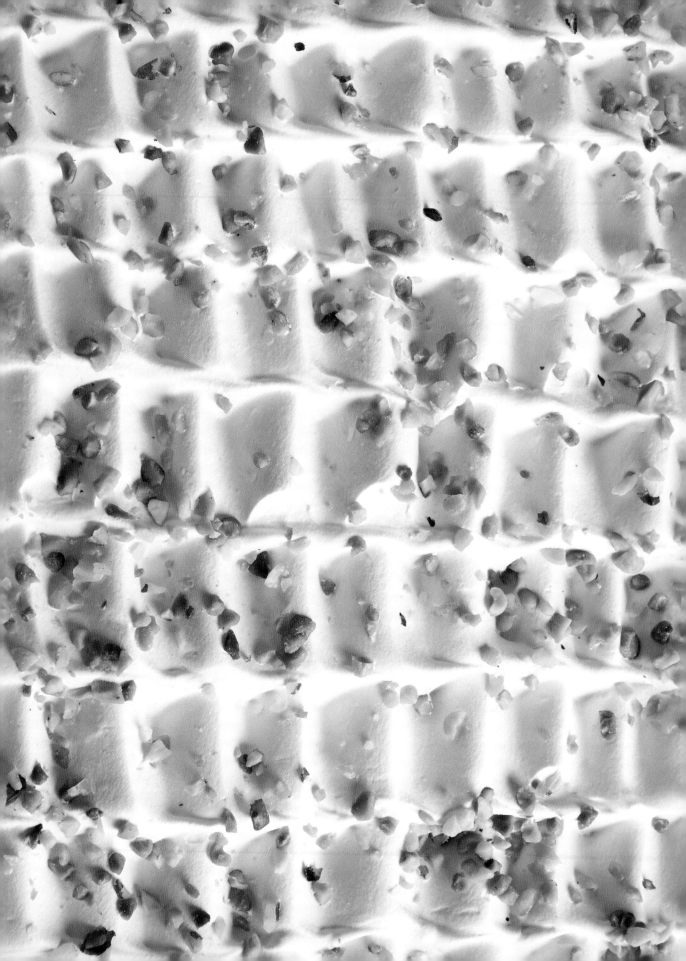

Chocolate Peanut Butter Torte

Makes one 9-by-13-inch torte

1 Nut Crust for Tortes (page 6)

6 cups whole milk

1½ cups cook-and-serve chocolate pudding powder

8 ounces cream cheese, softened

1¼ cups creamy peanut butter

2 cups powdered sugar

1 (16-ounce) container frozen whipped topping, thawed and divided

½ cup shelled salted peanuts, chopped

Whisk together the milk and pudding powder and cook over high heat until thick. Pour into a plastic container and refrigerate until cool.

Using the wire whisk attachment of an electric mixer, beat the cream cheese until softened. Add the peanut butter and mix. Add the sugar and mix. Fold in half the topping and mix again.

Spread the peanut butter mixture over the nut crust. Top with cooled pudding. Garnish with the remainder of the whipped topping and chopped peanuts.

Coconut Torte

Makes one 9-by-13-inch torte

• • • • • • • • • • • • •

1 Nut Crust for Tortes (page 6)

Cream Cheese Filling

8 ounces cream cheese, softened

2 cups powdered sugar

1 (8-ounce) container frozen whipped topping, thawed

Coconut Filling

1½ cups granulated sugar

¼ cup all-purpose flour

3 tablespoons cornstarch

1 cup flaked sweetened coconut

3 large egg yolks

3 cups whole milk

1 tablespoon salted butter

1 teaspoon vanilla extract

1 cup flaked sweetened coconut, toasted

1 (8-ounce) container frozen whipped topping, thawed, or Fresh Whipped Cream (page 17)

To make the cream cheese filling, mix the cream cheese with the sugar, using an electric stand mixer. Add the topping and mix until well blended and smooth.

Spread the crust with the cream cheese filling.

To make the coconut filling, combine the sugar, flour, cornstarch, and coconut in a saucepan and mix with a whisk. Add the egg yolks, but do not mix yet. Gradually add the milk, and stir all together thoroughly.

Cook over medium heat until thick and smooth, stirring constantly with a rubber spatula. Remove from heat. Add the butter and vanilla. Stir well and cool.

To toast the coconut, put the coconut in a pie pan and place it under the broiler for just a couple of minutes, watching closely and stirring occasionally, until golden brown.

Spread the coconut filling over the cream cheese filling. Top with the whipped topping or whipped cream and sprinkle with the toasted coconut.

Lemon Torte

Makes one 9-by-13-inch torte

1 Nut Crust for Tortes (page 6)

1 batch of Lemon Pudding (page 15)

Cream Cheese Filling

8 ounces cream cheese, softened

2 cups powdered sugar

1 (8-ounce) container frozen whipped topping, thawed

1 (8-ounce) container frozen whipped topping, thawed, or Fresh Whipped Cream (page 17)

To make the cream cheese filling, mix the cream cheese with the sugar, using an electric stand mixer. Add the topping and mix until well blended and smooth.

Spread the crust with the cream cheese filling, add a layer of lemon pudding, and top with whipped topping or whipped cream.

Chocolate Mint Torte

Makes one 9-by-13-inch torte

1 Nut Crust for Tortes (page 6)

1 batch of Chocolate Pudding (page 16)

8 ounces cream cheese, softened

2 cups powdered sugar

1 (16-ounce) container frozen whipped topping, thawed and divided

2 tablespoons crème de menthe

Green food coloring

Andes Candies, chopped

Using the wire whisk attachment of an electric stand mixer, beat the cream cheese. Add the sugar and mix. Add the crème de menthe and mix. Add half the whipped topping and mix. Spread the mixture on the crust. Top with chocolate pudding when it is completely cooled.

Mix the remainder of the whipped topping with 2 drops of green food coloring and spread evenly over the top of the chocolate pudding. Garnish with Andes candy pieces.

Pumpkin Torte

Makes one 9-by-13-inch torte

1 Graham Cracker Crust for Tortes (page 5)

2 cups pumpkin puree

1 cup granulated sugar, divided

1 teaspoon ground cinnamon

¼ teaspoon salt

½ cup whole milk

3 large egg yolks

3 large egg whites

1 individual envelope Knox unflavored gelatin powder

¼ cup cold water

1 (8-ounce) frozen whipped topping, thawed

In a large saucepan, combine the pumpkin puree, ½ cup of sugar, cinnamon, salt, milk, and egg yolks. Stir and cook over medium-high heat until thick.

Beat the egg whites until they are almost stiff. Add the other ½ cup of sugar and beat again.

Fold the egg whites into the pumpkin mixture. Cook until thick. Remove from heat.

Dissolve the gelatin powder in the water. Stir it into the pumpkin mixture. Cool. Pour the mixture over the crust. Refrigerate until set. Serve with whipped topping.

Rhubarb Torte

Makes one 9-by-13-inch torte

● ● ● ● ● ● ● ● ● ● ● ● ●

1 Nut Crust for Tortes (page 6)

½ cup (1 stick) salted butter

6 cups rhubarb, chopped

2 cups granulated sugar, divided

3 large egg yolks

½ cup half-and-half

½ cup all-purpose flour

Cream Cheese Filling

8 ounces cream cheese, softened

2 cups powdered sugar

1 (8-ounce) container frozen whipped topping, thawed

1 (8-ounce) container frozen whipped topping, thawed

In a large saucepan, melt the butter over low heat. Add the rhubarb and cook until the rhubarb is coated with butter. Add 1½ cups sugar and cook until soft.

In a separate bowl, mix the egg yolks, half-and-half, ½ cup sugar, and flour until smooth. Add to the hot rhubarb mixture. Cook until thick. Refrigerate.

To make the cream cheese filling, mix the cream cheese with the sugar, using an electric stand mixer. Add the topping and mix until well blended and smooth.

Spread the crust with the cream cheese mixture. When the rhubarb mixture is set, add it over the cream cheese layer. Top with the other container of whipped topping.

MUFFINS

Cranberry Orange Muffins

Makes 1 dozen muffins

2 cups all-purpose flour

1 tablespoon baking powder

½ teaspoon salt

¾ cup granulated sugar

1 large egg

¾ cup orange juice

1 teaspoon grated orange rind

¼ cup vegetable oil

1 cup cranberries, halved

Preheat the oven to 400 degrees.

Butter or spray the 12 molds of a regular-size muffin pan, or fit the molds with paper muffin cups.

In a large bowl, stir together the flour, baking powder, salt, and sugar. Make a well in the center of the mixture.

In a small bowl or a 2-cup measuring cup, beat the egg with a fork. Stir in the orange juice, orange rind, and oil. Pour this mixture into the well in the dry mixture. Mix quickly and lightly with a fork until moistened, but do not beat. The batter will be lumpy. Fold in cranberries. Divide the batter evenly among the muffin cups.

Bake for 25 minutes, or until the tops are golden brown and a thin knife inserted into the center of the muffins comes out clean. Transfer the pan to a rack and cool for 5 minutes before carefully removing each muffin from its mold. Store the muffins in an airtight container at room temperature.

Raisin Bran Muffins

Makes 18 to 20 muffins

Tip:

To plump the raisins, boil them in just enough water to cover the raisins for about 1 minute and drain the water. This adds moisture to the raisins and will give you a moister muffin.

2 cups all-purpose flour

1 cup granulated sugar

2½ teaspoons baking soda

¾ teaspoon salt

½ cup vegetable oil

2 large eggs

2 cups buttermilk

2 cups bran flakes

1½ cups raisins, plumped

Preheat the oven to 400 degrees.

Butter or spray 18 to 20 molds of 2 regular-size muffin pans, or fit the molds with paper muffin cups.

In a large bowl, stir together the flour, sugar, baking soda, and salt. Add the oil, eggs, and buttermilk and mix. Add the bran flakes and raisins and stir. Do not overmix. Fill the muffin cups almost full.

Bake for about 25 to 30 minutes, or until the tops are golden brown and a thin knife inserted into the center of the muffins comes out clean. Transfer the pan to a rack and cool for 5 minutes before carefully removing each muffin from its mold. Store the muffins in an airtight container at room temperature.

Lemon Poppy Seed Muffins

Makes 1 dozen muffins

⅔ cup granulated sugar

Grated rind and juice of 1 lemon

2 cups all-purpose flour

2 teaspoons baking powder

¼ teaspoon baking soda

¼ teaspoon salt

¾ cup sour cream

2 large eggs

1 teaspoon vanilla extract

½ cup (1 stick) salted butter, melted and cooled

2 tablespoons poppy seeds

Preheat the oven to 400 degrees.

Butter or spray the 12 molds of a regular-size muffin pan, or fit the molds with paper muffin cups.

In a large bowl, rub the sugar and lemon rind together with your fingertips until the sugar is moist and the fragrance of lemon strong. Whisk in the flour, baking powder, baking soda, and salt.

In a large glass measuring cup or another bowl, whisk together the sour cream, eggs, vanilla, lemon juice, and butter until well blended. Pour the liquid ingredients over the dry ingredients and, with the whisk or a rubber spatula, gently but quickly stir to blend. Don't worry about being thorough—a few lumps are better than overmixing the batter. Stir in the poppy seeds. Divide the batter evenly among the muffin cups.

Bake for 18 to 20 minutes, or until the tops are golden brown and a thin knife inserted into the center of the muffins comes out clean. Transfer the pan to a rack and cool for 5 minutes before carefully removing each muffin from its mold. Store the muffins in an airtight container at room temperature.

Blueberry Muffins

2 cups all-purpose flour

1 tablespoon baking powder

½ teaspoon salt

¾ cup granulated sugar

1 large egg

¾ cup whole milk

¼ cup vegetable oil

1 cup blueberries

Preheat the oven to 400 degrees.

Butter or spray the 12 molds of a regular-size muffin pan, or fit the molds with paper muffin cups.

In a large bowl, stir together the flour, baking powder, salt, and sugar. Make a well in the center of the mixture.

In a small bowl or a 2-cup measuring cup, beat the egg with a fork. Stir in the milk and oil. Pour this mixture into the well of the dry mixture. Mix quickly and lightly with a fork until moistened, but do not beat. The batter will be lumpy. Fold in the blueberries. Divide the batter evenly among the muffin cups.

Bake for 25 minutes, or until the tops are golden brown and a thin knife inserted into the center of the muffins comes out clean. Transfer the pan to a rack and cool for 5 minutes before carefully removing each muffin from its mold. Store the muffins in an airtight container at room temperature.

Four Berry Cream Cheese Muffins

Makes 1 dozen muffins

Cream Cheese Mixure and Berries

4 ounces cream cheese, softened

¼ cup powdered sugar

1 tablespoon Norske Nook Four Berry Jam

Muffin Batter

2 cups all-purpose flour

1 tablespoon baking powder

½ teaspoon salt

1 large egg

1 cup whole milk

½ cup granulated sugar, plus additional for sprinkling

1 teaspoon vanilla extract

4 tablespoons salted butter, melted

¼ cup Norske Nook Four Berry Jam

Preheat the oven to 400 degrees.

Butter or spray the 12 molds of a regular-size muffin pan, or fit the molds with paper muffin cups.

To make the cream cheese mixture, mix the cream cheese with the sugar in a medium bowl. Make sure the cream cheese is room temperature, which will prevent lumps. Add the jam and mix.

To make the batter, mix the flour, baking powder, and salt in another bowl and set aside. Beat the egg in a separate bowl, then add the milk, sugar, and vanilla to the egg. Combine the egg and flour mixtures. Add the butter and mix, being careful not to overmix. The batter will be a little lumpy.

Using only half the muffin batter, spoon the batter evenly among the muffin cups. Add 1 teaspoon of the cream cheese mixure on top of the batter, in the middle. Place 1 teaspoon of jam on top of the cream cheese. Distribute the other half of the batter among the cups. Sprinkle with sugar.

Bake for 20 to 25 minutes, or until the tops are golden brown and a thin knife inserted into the center of the muffins comes out clean. Transfer the pan to a rack and cool for 5 minutes before carefully removing each muffin from its mold. Store the muffins in an airtight container at room temperature.

Strawberry Cream Cheese Muffins

Makes 1 dozen muffins

Strawberry Mixture

1 cup strawberries, sliced

½ cup granulated sugar

¾ cup water

4 tablespoons cornstarch

4 tablespoons cold water

Cream Cheese Mixture

4 ounces cream cheese, softened

¼ cup powdered sugar

Muffin Batter

2 cups all-purpose flour

1 tablespoon baking powder

½ teaspoon salt

1 large egg

½ cup granulated sugar, plus additional for sprinkling

1 cup whole milk

1 teaspoon vanilla extract

4 tablespoons salted butter, melted

Preheat the oven to 400 degrees.

Butter or spray the 12 molds of a regular-size muffin pan, or fit the molds with paper muffin cups.

To make the strawberry mixture, boil the strawberries, sugar, and water together. Mix the cornstarch with cold water. (Make sure to use cold water.) Add the cornstarch mix to the boiling mixture. Boil until the mixture is clear and thick, which will not take long. Cool the mixture.

To make the cream cheese mixture, mix the cream cheese with the sugar in a bowl. Make sure the cream cheese is room temperature, which will prevent lumps.

To make the batter, mix the flour, baking powder, and salt in another bowl and set aside. Beat the egg in a separate bowl, then add the sugar, milk, and vanilla to the egg. Combine the egg and flour mixtures. Add the butter and mix, being careful not to overmix. The batter will be a little lumpy.

Using only half the muffin batter, spoon the batter evenly among the muffin cups. Add 1 teaspoon of the cream cheese mixture on top of the batter, in the middle. Place 1 teaspoon of the strawberries on top of the cream cheese. Distribute the other half of the batter among the cups. Sprinkle with sugar.

Bake for 20 to 25 minutes, or until the tops are golden brown and a thin knife inserted into the center of the muffins comes out clean. Transfer the pan to a rack and cool for 5 minutes before carefully removing each muffin from its mold. Store the muffins in an airtight container at room temperature.

Any extra strawberry mixture makes great topping for toast or ice cream.

COOKIES

MOM, COUSIN CARRIE, AND DELICIOUS COOKIES

When I was young, my mother would take me to town to visit one of her elderly Norwegian distant cousins who lived in an apartment on the second floor of a large house. Her name was Carrie, and she would bake goods out of her home to sell to the corner grocery store. Carrie would always greet me with a warm hug and traditional kiss on the cheek. I loved going there because she was always baking and I loved the smell of baked goods—it was heaven to me at four years old. I especially enjoyed the huge sour cream cookie she'd give me to eat while I watched Captain Kangaroo, Bozo, or Sheriff Bob on TV.

As I have said, my mom loved to cook and was thrilled to make the cookies and cakes that my dad loved. He really enjoyed oatmeal cookies, date-filled cookies, and, of course, gingerbread cookies. He would dunk them in his coffee and pack some in the old metal lunch box that he took to work at the Uniroyal Tire factory. I loved it when he came home and I would sit on his lap before he headed out to the barn to feed the cattle or to work in the field. With one arm he'd hold me, with the other he'd be dipping cookies into his coffee, and occasionally he'd let me steal a bite.

Like all good moms, my mom would let us kids lick the spatulas, spoons, and mixing bowls between batches, and of course she'd make us wash them before the next batch. One day she was baking dozens and dozens of cookies. After I licked the spoon she had just used to mix the gingerbread cookies, I decided I would eat a few handfuls of the cookie dough while she had her back turned. (I'm not just a jokester, I'm also a rocket scientist!) Of course, I got caught after I'd eaten most of the dough, and she was very upset with me. While she was yelling at me, which at the time seemed like an eternity, I got sick, which made her stop being upset and feel bad for me, and she nursed me back to health. When I'd recovered a few days later, I couldn't eat gingerbread cookies or go near the kitchen when she was making them. It was close to twenty-five years before I could eat or bake gingerbread cookies! But now, I love the smell of freshly baked gingerbread cookies again.

—Jerry Bechard

Sour Cream Sugar Cookies

Makes about 2 dozen cookies

4½ cups all-purpose flour

½ teaspoon salt

1 teaspoon baking soda

1 teaspoon baking powder

1 cup (2 sticks) salted butter, softened

1¾ cups granulated sugar

2 large eggs

1 tablespoon vanilla extract

1 cup sour cream

Preheat the oven to 325 degrees.

In a small bowl, combine the flour, salt, baking soda, and baking powder. Set aside.

Using an electric mixer and a large bowl, beat the butter and sugar until creamy. Add the eggs and vanilla and mix well. Add the sour cream and mix well. Gradually add the flour mixture and mix well.

Cool the uncovered bowl of dough in the refrigerator for 30 minutes.

Roll out the dough ¼-inch thick. Using a large round cookie cutter, cut dough circles and place them onto greased cookie sheets.

Bake until the cookies are golden brown on the edges, about 15 minutes. Cool completely and store in an airtight container.

Molasses Gingerbread Cookies

Makes about 4 dozen cookies

• • • • • • • • • • • • •

¾ cup (1½ sticks) salted butter or shortening

1½ cups granulated sugar, plus additional for sprinkling

¾ cup molasses

2 large eggs

1 tablespoon baking soda

¼ cup hot water

1 teaspoon ground ginger

1 teaspoon ground cinnamon

4 cups all-purpose flour

Preheat the oven to 375 degrees.

Using an electric mixer, beat the shortening and sugar together in a large bowl, then add the molasses and mix. Push the dough to the side of the bowl. Add the eggs and slightly beat them with a whisk before mixing them in. Dissolve the baking soda in the hot water, add it to the dough, and blend well.

Add the ginger, cinnamon, and flour, and mix well, using a wooden spoon. Cover the dough with plastic wrap and refrigerate for about 2 hours.

Flatten the dough on a floured board or table, roll it out with a rolling pin, and cut it into desired shapes with a cookie cutter.

Sprinkle sugar over a cookie sheet pan. Place the cutouts on the cookie sheet and sprinkle tops with sugar.

Bake for 10 minutes. Cool completely, then decorate and sprinkle more sugar on top. Store in an airtight container.

Chocolate Chip Cookies

Makes about 4 dozen cookies

½ cup (1 stick) salted butter, softened

½ cup butter flavor Crisco

½ cup granulated sugar

1½ cups packed light brown sugar

2 large eggs

2 teaspoons vanilla extract

2¾ cups (12 ounces) all-purpose flour (weigh the flour if possible)

1 teaspoon baking soda

1½ teaspoons baking powder

¾ teaspoon small- to medium-grain coarse sea salt

2¼ cups semisweet chocolate chips

Preheat the oven to 350 degrees.

Using an electric mixer, beat the butter, Crisco, and both sugars until nice and fluffy, about 3 minutes on medium-high speed. Add the eggs and vanilla and beat for an additional 2 minutes. Combine the flour, baking soda, baking powder, and salt in a separate bowl and mix them into the cookie batter. Finally, add the chocolate chips until well distributed throughout. The cookie batter should be somewhat thick.

Drop 2-tablespoon scoops of dough onto a baking sheet lined with parchment paper.

Bake for 12 to 14 minutes, until the edges are nice and golden brown. Remove from heat and leave the cookies on the cookie sheet for an additional 2 minutes. Pick up the parchment paper with the cookies still on top and transfer to a cool, nonporous surface. Allow the cookies to cool on the paper for at least 3 minutes before serving. Store in an airtight container.

Poppy Seed Cookies

Makes about 3 dozen cookies

• • • • • • • • • • • • •

1¼ cups (2½ sticks) salted butter, softened

1¼ cup granulated sugar

1¼ cup powdered sugar

9 large egg yolks

½ teaspoon vanilla extract

½ cup poppy seeds

4½ cups all-purpose flour

¼ teaspoon salt

Preheat the oven to 350 degrees.

Using an electric stand mixer, beat the butter and both sugars. Add the egg yolks, vanilla, and poppy seeds and mix well. Add the flour and salt. Mix well.

Drop heaping tablespoons of dough onto a greased cookie sheet.

Bake until light brown around the edges. Baking times will vary. Cool completely and store in an airtight container.

Oatmeal Date-Filled Cookies

Makes about 3 to 4 dozen cookies

Filling

2 cups dates, chopped

½ cup granulated sugar

1 cup water

Cookies

10 cups all-purpose flour

4 cups light brown sugar

8 cups old-fashioned or quick-cooking rolled oats

4 teaspoons baking soda

4 teaspoons salt

4 cups (8 sticks) salted butter, softened

2½ cups water

Preheat the oven to 375 degrees.

Make the filling first. Combine the dates, sugar, and water in a medium saucepan on medium heat, and cook until thick. Be careful not to burn. Watch closely, and stir often. Remove from the heat, and allow to cool.

You can keep the filling in a tightly covered container in the refrigerator until ready to use.

To make the cookies, in a large bowl, combine the flour, sugar, oatmeal, baking soda, and salt and mix with your hands. Add the butter to the dry mixture and mix until the butter is incorporated. Add the water and mix again. Take a small amount of dough at a time and roll out to about ¼ inch thick. Using a round cookie cutter, cut dough circles and place them on a dry, clean sheet pan. Put a 1-tablespoon scoop of the date filling in the middle of each dough circle, and the fold the cookie in half to cover the date filling.

Bake until golden brown, about 10 minutes. Cool completely and store in an airtight container.

Peanut Butter Cookies

Makes about 5 dozen cookies

● ● ● ● ● ● ● ● ● ● ● ●

1 cup (2 sticks) salted butter, softened

1 cup butter flavor Crisco

1 cup granulated sugar

1 cup light brown sugar

1 cup creamy peanut butter

2 large eggs

1 cup old-fashioned rolled oats (not quick-cooking)

2 tablespoons baking soda

½ teaspoon salt

2 cups all-purpose flour

1 bag (2 cups) peanut butter chips

Preheat the oven to 350 degrees.

Using an electric stand mixer, combine the butter, Crisco, both sugars, and peanut butter. Add the eggs and oats and mix. Scrape down the sides of the mixer and along the bottom. Add baking soda, salt, and flour and mix. Add the peanut butter chips and stir. Add more flour if the dough is too sticky.

Using a ¼ cup scoop and flattening the dough against your palm to get a level scoop, drop the scoops onto a greased cookie sheet. Flatten with a fork.

Bake for 12 minutes, until lightly brown around the edges. Cool completely and store in an airtight container.

Spritz Cookies

Makes about 3 dozen small cookies

* * * * * * * * * * * * *

1½ cups (3 sticks) salted butter, softened

1 cup granulated sugar

1 large egg

1 teaspoon vanilla extract

½ teaspoon almond extract

4 cups sifted all-purpose flour

1 teaspoon baking powder

Preheat the oven to 400 degrees.

Using a stand mixer, thoroughly mix together the butter and sugar. Add the egg, vanilla, and almond extract and beat well. Sift together the flour and baking powder, then gradually add this mixture to the butter mixture, mixing until the dough is smooth.

Roll the dough into 1-inch balls and flatten them on an ungreased cookie sheet.

Bake for about 8 to 10 minutes. Sprinkle with sugar. Cool completely and store in an airtight container.

Norwegian Pepper Cookies

Makes about 18 cookies

Cookies

½ cup (1 stick) salted butter, softened

½ cup granulated sugar

2 tablespoons whipping cream

½ teaspoon baking soda

2 tablespoons water

1½ cups plus 2 tablespoons all-purpose flour

½ teaspoon baking powder

¾ teaspoon ground cardamom

½ teaspoon ground cinnamon

½ teaspoon ground black pepper

Lemon Glaze

2 cups sifted powdered sugar

3 tablespoons lemon juice

Preheat the oven to 375 degrees.

Using a stand mixer on high speed, beat the butter and sugar until light and fluffy. Add the cream, baking soda, and water until thoroughly combined.

Sift together the flour, baking powder, and spices and add to the butter mixture. On a low speed, beat until the dough is fully combined.

Turn the dough out onto the counter and shape it into a roll about 2½ inches in diameter. Wrap it tightly in plastic wrap and chill the dough thoroughly, approximately 2 hours.

Cut the chilled dough into thin slices, and gently smooth each into a round. Roll in granulated sugar to evenly coat the dough.

Bake on a parchment-lined cookie sheet for 6 to 8 minutes, until lightly browned around the edges. Let the cookies cool for several minutes before moving them to wire racks.

To make the glaze, mix together the sugar and lemon juice until smooth and spreadable. If the mixture is too stiff, add another tablespoon of lemon juice. Brush the cooled cookies with the glaze and let stand at room temperature until the glaze is set. Store in an airtight container.

Oatmeal Raisin Cookies

Makes about 4 dozen cookies

2 cups raisins

1 cup water

½ cup (1 stick) salted butter

½ cup butter flavor Crisco

2 cups granulated sugar

1 teaspoon vanilla extract

3 large eggs

2 cups old-fashioned rolled oats (not quick-cooking)

2 cups all-purpose flour

1 teaspoon baking powder

1 teaspoon baking soda

1½ teaspoons ground cinnamon

¼ teaspoon ground nutmeg

¼ teaspoon ground allspice

½ teaspoon salt

Preheat the oven to 375 degrees.

In a small saucepan, boil the raisins in water for 5 minutes or so, drain, and save 5 tablespoons of the raisin juice. Let cool.

Using an electric stand mixer, mix together the butter, Crisco, and sugar. Add the vanilla, eggs, and the cooled raisin juice and mix.

In a separate bowl, mix together the oats, flour, baking powder, baking soda, spices, and salt. Blend well with the raisin mixture and drop rounded teaspoons of dough onto a lightly buttered cookie sheet.

Bake for 12 to 15 minutes, until a finger doesn't leave a dent. They will have rounded tops. Cool completely and store in an airtight container.

Velkommen

til

Norske Nook

Please wait to be seated

SCANDINAVIAN
SPECIALTIES

· ·

Scandinavian Rosettes

Makes about 40 rosettes

2 large eggs

2 teaspoons granulated sugar

¼ teaspoon salt

1 cup whole milk

1 cup all-purpose flour

Enough peanut oil for a deep fryer to be ¾ full

1 cup granulated sugar

You will need a rosette iron, available at www.norskenook.com and elsewhere.

Beat the eggs a little with the sugar and salt. Add the milk and flour and beat until smooth. Let the mixture rest before frying.

Heat the oil in the fryer. Rosettes are delicate; you'll have to test the temperature a bit. If the grease is too hot, the outside of the rosettes will fry too fast and the middle will be soggy. If the grease isn't hot enough the whole rosette will be soggy.

Dip the iron into the hot oil. Remove from the oil and shake off the grease. Dip the iron into the batter (but don't let the batter cover the top of the iron). Submerge the battered iron in the oil completely and cook until a light golden brown. Remove from the oil and shake off the excess grease, and carefully loosen the rosette from the iron, using a fork. Remove the rosette from the iron and lay on paper toweling. Put the sugar in a shallow bowl, and when the rosette has cooled, dip it in sugar.

Lefse

8 large baking potatoes, peeled and cut into wedges
3 tablespoons salted butter, softened
½ cup half-and-half
Pinch of salt
1 cup all-purpose flour

You will need a lefse grill, corrugated lefse rolling pin, lefse stick, and pastry board and cloth set, all available at www.norskenook.com and elsewhere.

Preheat the lefse grill to 375 degrees.

Boil the potatoes in a large pot of water until tender. Drain.

Using an electric stand mixer, use paddles to mix the potatoes, butter, half-and-half, and salt in a large bowl until well blended and creamy. Or you can press the potatoes through a potato ricer. If you have a potato ricer, first press the potatoes through the ricer, then mix with the other ingredients.

Using a large wooden mixing spoon, fold the flour a third at a time into the potato mixture until it forms a firm, non-sticky dough. You may need a little extra or a little less flour depending on the moisture in the potatoes. Fold the flour into the potato mixture—don't stir it. These aren't made the same way as mashed potatoes.

Divide the dough and, using your hands, roll it into 24 balls about the size of golf balls. Place each one on a generously floured board (preferably one covered with rolling cloth designed for making lefse), and gently pat the top with your hand to flatten slightly. Using a rolling pin designed for lefse, roll the dough until it's quite thin, about ¼ inch, and almost translucent. When rolling the dough for each piece of lefse, be careful to make the outer edges as thin as the rest of the dough.

Gently slide a lefse stick under the rolled dough to loosen all the way around. Now, slide the stick under the middle of the dough and raise it off the floured board. Carry the dough on the stick to the heated lefse grill (or a cast-iron skillet), and carefully ease the dough onto the grill by rolling the stick to one side.

Cook for about 3 minutes, or until golden brown spots begin to form. Flip over using the lefse stick and cook an additional 3 minutes, or until the lefse has formed golden air bubbles. Use the lefse stick to remove the finished piece from the grill and place it on a towel to cool.

Repeat until all the dough has been used.

If too much flour builds up on the hot lefse griddle, it takes longer for the lefse to cook. Be sure to keep the surface of the grill clean.

The lefse is wonderful eaten immediately, warm, or at room temperature with butter and sugar. Once cooled, store it in an airtight container in a cool place.

Krumkaka

Makes about 4 dozen cookies

¼ cup (½ stick) salted butter, softened

1 cup granulated sugar

2 large eggs

1 cup heavy whipping cream

½ cup whole milk

3 tablespoons vanilla extract

1½ cups all-purpose flour

You will need an electric krumkaka iron, available at www.norskenook.com and elsewhere.

With an electric stand mixer, combine the butter and sugar. Add the eggs and mix. Add the cream, milk, and vanilla and mix. Add the flour and mix. Refrigerate for 2 hours or overnight.

Heat the krumkaka iron on medium heat. Put about a teaspoon of batter on the bottom of the iron and press the top and bottom of the iron together (much like a waffle iron or sandwich press). When brown on one side, turn the krumkaka over and brown again.

When the krumkaka is done, remove it from the iron and roll it around the cone form. It does not take long. You do not want it to be dark brown or broken. Repeat until all the dough has been used.

Rommegrot Norwegian Pudding

Makes 12 cups

½ gallon heavy whipping cream

½ cup powdered sugar

1 tablespoon vanilla extract

1 cup all-purpose flour

½ cup (1 stick) salted butter, melted

1 tablespoon ground cinnamon

¼ cup granulated sugar

Combine the cream, powdered sugar, and vanilla in a sauce-pan over high heat and stir. When the mixture is hot, start whisking in the flour. Continue cooking until thickened, approximately 10 to 15 minutes. Pour into a crock pot. Add butter and sprinkle with cinnamon sugar to serve.

Scandinavian Oatmeal Flat Bread

Makes about 40 (16-inch) squares

● ● ● ● ● ● ● ● ● ● ● ●

Tip:

You can replace 1 cup of all-purpose flour with 1 cup of wheat flour for a slightly darker flatbread.

4 cups quick-cooking rolled oats

½ cup granulated sugar

2 teaspoons baking soda

1 teaspoon salt

1½ cups (3 sticks) salted butter, melted

3 cups buttermilk

5 cups all-purpose flour

Preheat the oven to 350 degrees.

Mix the oats, sugar, baking soda, and salt together in a large bowl. Add the butter and mix. Add the buttermilk and the flour and mix. (You may need more flour for rolling.)

On a floured board, take a piece of dough about the size of an egg and roll it very thin (paper thin) using a grooved rolling pin.

Bake on an ungreased cookie sheet for about 10 minutes, until firm and slightly brown.

Scandinavian Sandbakkels

Makes about 6 dozen sandbakkels

½ cup (1 stick) salted butter, softened

½ cup white Crisco

1 cup granulated sugar

1 teaspoon vanilla extract

2 large eggs

½ teaspoon salt

3 cups all-purpose flour

You will need sandbakkel tins, similar to tart tins, available at www.norskenook.com and elsewhere.

Preheat the oven to 350 degrees.

Using an electric stand mixer, combine the butter and Crisco. Add the sugar and vanilla and mix, then add the eggs, 1 at a time. Add the salt and flour and continue mixing.

Press the batter thinly into bakkel tins, *not* thick. Place the tins on a cookie sheet.

Bake for 25 to 30 minutes, until golden brown like a pie crust. Watch closely so they do not burn. Sandbakkels are buttery and fragile.

Almond Cake

Makes one cake that
serves 12

● ● ● ● ● ● ● ● ● ● ● ● ●

1¼ cups granulated sugar

1 large egg

⅔ cup whole milk

1½ teaspoons almond extract

½ teaspoon baking powder

1¼ cups all-purpose flour

½ cup (1 stick) salted butter, melted

Powdered sugar for sprinkling

You will need an almond cake pan, available at
www.norskenook.com and elsewhere.

Preheat the oven to 350 degrees.

Mix the ingredients in the order they are listed, being careful not to overbeat.

Bake in the almond cake pan for 1 hour and 15 minutes. The
edges should be golden brown. The cake will break apart if
you remove it too soon.

After the cake has cooled, sprinkle it with powdered sugar.

Special Tools

All items listed here are available for purchase at www.norskenook.com and elsewhere.

almond cake pan: A rectangular nonstick pan with a fluted bottom, usually about 12 inches by 4 inches, used for making perfect almond cakes.

corrugated rolling pin: A pin with special grooves that helps get lefse dough to the proper thinness.

krumkaka iron: Much like a waffle iron, used for baking two very thin, traditional Scandinavian cookies at a time.

lefse grill: A specialty appliance that reaches the high temperatures for making perfect lefse.

lefse stick: Sometimes called a lefse turner, used for transferring lefse dough from the workspace to the lefse grill.

Norske Nook pie filling: Delicious alternatives to making your own filling. We proudly sell all varieties listed in our pie recipes, and you can feel confident using them in your pies and desserts.

pie tin: At Norske Nook, a round metal pie pan, 11 inches in diameter, used for baking pies.

rosette iron: A utensil in two pieces, a long metal handle and a decorative cast-iron form, used to dip batter in oil to fry it into shapes.

sandbakkel tins: A set of tins that mold the shapes and properly bake the Scandinavian sandbakkel cookies.

Acknowledgments

Without Helen Myhre and her staff of knowledgeable and talented bakers, cooks, and waitresses training me to join the fantastic world of the Norske Nook, I would not be here twenty-five years later writing this cookbook. Through her initial guidance and direction, and of course all of her staff, some of whom still work here, we have been able to successfully maintain that small rural café-style home cooking in all of our locations, and expand our line of tasty pies and desserts. I cannot thank them enough.

I would like to give special thanks to my cowriter and regional manager, Cindee Borton-Parker, and my bakery manger, Kim Hanson. Special thanks also to the original staff who have been with me from the beginning: Fredricka (Flicka) Torpen, Shari Brown, Linda Gunderson, Marlene Hagen, and my sister in-law Judy Bechard for their guidance and advice, and thanks to all of those who started with me and struggled alongside me over the years to maintain the Norske Nook's identity and experience for our loyal customers.

I would also like to thank my two children, Adam Bechard and Laura Bechard, and my other extended family members for putting up with the long hours I spent working to get things just right at the Nook, and encouraging me to finally put all of these exciting recipes together for this book.

Thanks also to my mother, Darleen Bechard, and my sisters, Anita Canfield and Judy Burce, for inspiring me while they allowed me to lick the spoons with them when they were cooking when I was a young boy growing up on a small farm in rural Wisconsin.

—Jerry Bechard

First and foremost I would like to thank Jerry Bechard for being the best leader, for trusting me to be a part of this project, and for his endless generosity and friendship. Thanks to all the incredible bakers, staff, and managers of the Norske Nook for their constant dedication, with an immense thanks to Shari Brown, Heidi Myron-Becker, Jean Zingshiem, Sara Zeiler, Joni Shields, Stacy Campbell, Kim Hanson, and Mariel Martinez for all the extra efforts in helping with this book.

An enormous thank you to my niece Beth Wankel for her hours of assistance and self-sacrifice helping me with this book, and to my husband, Larry Parker, for putting up with my not coming to bed at night due to typing recipes into the early morning hours, and for always willing to be my pie taster. Thanks also to my mother, Judy Borton, for her unconditional love and constant encouragement and offerings of help, and to my son, Beau Fenske, for always being my reason.

And of course big thanks to Executive Editor Raphael Kadushin for taking on this project and for his eye for detail and patience. Thanks as well to the other UW Press staff, especially Andrea Christofferson and the rest of the marketing department for spreading the word about the book and Sheila McMahon for expertly guiding us through the process and creating the index. And thanks to Rose Design for the beautiful layout of the book and cover.

Thanks also to Mette Nielsen for the amazing photography and Cindy Syme for the styling; they both were such a joy to work with.

—Cindee Borton-Parker

Biographies

Jerry Bechard was born in Eau Claire, Wisconsin, and raised on a farm outside of Chippewa Falls. He attended the University of Wisconsin–Eau Claire and graduated from Metro State College in Denver, Colorado, with a bachelor's degree in criminal justice.

In the late 1970s Jerry became an assistant manager of a Perkins Restaurant in Madison, Wisconsin. Later he became a general manager of Perkins restaurants in Utah and Colorado. At that time he was the youngest manager ever employed by Perkins.

Jerry then switched careers and worked through the ranks as a police officer in Colorado. While working in law enforcement he took up the hobby of home brewing, making small batches of beer for his friends and family. It was around this time that he returned to Wisconsin and purchased the Norske Nook restaurant from Helen Myhre.

For twenty-five years Jerry has owned the Norske Nook, which with the help of the staff has grown from one small café to four locations, and has increased the pie repertoire from twenty to more than seventy varieties. Jerry has also opened Northwoods Brewing and Northwoods Brewpub and Grill, which serves some of his own beer recipes and a full selection of Norske Nook pies.

Jerry and his crew have earned thirty-six blue ribbons for their pies in competition at the National Pie Championships, sponsored by the American Pie Council. After numerous requests from diners, he and his staff decided to release a cookbook, with recipes for their pies and other baked goods.

Cindee Borton-Parker is the pie-loving regional manager for the Norske Nook restaurants and bakeries in northwest Wisconsin.

Cindee's food service career began when she was just thirteen years old, working alongside her mother at a small-town café. Since then she has worked in almost every area of the restaurant business. You could say it's in her genes; it's what she knows and loves.

In 2001, Cindee was hired as assistant general manager of the Norske Nook in Rice Lake. In 2002, she became general manager of that location, and in 2007 she moved up to multiunit regional manager and continued her education in supervisory management.

Cindee works diligently to ensure that Norske Nook upholds the integrity of its traditions and award-winning, time-honored recipes, pies "made from scratch, each crust rolled by hand." She takes pride in all of Norske Nook's food, but pays careful attention to the taste, quality, and presentation of the famous pies. If the pie isn't award-winning quality, it doesn't get served.

Cindee enjoys creating new recipes with the bakers, and being the lucky taste tester for the pies. She also consults with brides and grooms about serving pies at their wedding in place of cake. Pie pairs perfectly with weddings!

Cindee is the one expected to bring Norske Nook pie to all social gatherings and family events.

Index